The

BENEDICTINE NUNS
& KYLEMORE ABBEY

a history

Deirdre Raftery is Professor of the History of Education at University College Dublin, and an elected Fellow of the Royal Historical Society. She has thirteen book publications, including *Nano Nagle: The Life and the Legacy* (Irish Academic Press, 2018).

Catherine KilBride was Principal of Pembroke School (Miss Meredith's), Education Director of the Marketing Institute, and lecturer in Education Management at University College Dublin. She is now an editor, translator and writer. This is her fourth book.

The

BENEDICTINE NUNS
& KYLEMORE ABBEY

a history

DEIRDRE RAFTERY & CATHERINE KILBRIDE

MERRION
PRESS

First published in hardback in 2020 by
Irish Academic Press
10 George's Street
Newbridge
Co. Kildare
Ireland
www.merrionpress.ie

This paperback edition first published by Merrion Press in 2024

9781788551731 (Paperback)
9781788551526 (Ebook)

A CIP catalogue record for this book is available from the British Library.

Unless otherwise stated, all images are courtesy of the Kylemore Abbey Archives,
except pp. 28–37, 60–79, 112–29, 160–71 and 198–9, where images are
courtesy of Michelle Cooper-Galvin and Diarmuid Galvin.

Design and setting: edit+ www.stuartcoughlan.com
Cover design: edit+ www.stuartcoughlan.com
Typeset in Adobe Garamond Pro

Merrion Press is a member of Publishing Ireland.

CONTENTS

THE BENEDICTINE NUNS

1920 2020

JUSTUS ET FIDELIS

PAX

KYLEMORE ABBEY CENTENARY

PREFACE

This book provides an account of the Irish Benedictines and Kylemore Abbey. While the book locates the history of this monastery within wider Benedictine history, reaching back to the seventh century, it pays particular attention to how the 'Irish Dames' were first established in 1665. Their monastery in Ypres, founded at a time when Catholics in Ireland were being persecuted for their faith, became a place that educated generations of Irish girls and women. When the Irish Dames of Ypres were forced to leave Belgium during the First World War, they made their way to Ireland – firstly to Wexford, and then to what would become their permanent home in Connemara.

The book is based on research at Kylemore Abbey Archives, the National Archives of Ireland and the National Library of Ireland. It attempts an evidence-based account of the history of the Irish Benedictines, of their journey to Kylemore and of the hundred years they have spent there. A serious difficulty for any scholar working on the history of the Ypres monastery is that archival records were destroyed during the First Battle of Ypres; only a handful of treasures were saved from the monastery. The nuns, however, kept a journal as they travelled from Ypres in 1914 to Kylemore in 1920. Useful sources for the Kylemore part of this book were the Council Minutes, Chapter Minutes and extant records of Kylemore Abbey School. These, together with official publications from the Department of Education and selected newspaper records, have been used to create a picture of life at Kylemore Abbey over the past century.

The book is illustrated throughout with images from the Kylemore Abbey Archives. Between the chapters there are thematically organised collections of photographs which were specially commissioned for this volume. For this, our sincere thanks go to Michelle Cooper-Galvin and Diarmuid Galvin. The themes are derived from the four Benedictine mottoes: Pax (peace), Ora (prayer), Labora (work) and Succisa Virescit, which suggests the regrowth and renewal at Kylemore about which Mother Abbess Máire Hickey writes in the Epilogue.

We greatly appreciated the warm Benedictine hospitality of Mother Máire Hickey and the community at Kylemore Abbey during the research. Our gratitude is extended to Dr Damien Duffy, Kylemore Abbey Archivist, and to Dr Catriona Delaney, ConventCollections Fellow, UCD. Permission to cite letters from the Presentation Sisters Congregational Archives, George's Hill, Dublin, is gratefully acknowledged.

Deirdre Raftery and Catherine KilBride

GLOSSARY

Abbess/Abbot The title given to the Superior of a Benedictine abbey. Historically, once elected, a Superior served for life. The Second Vatican Council (1962–5) ruled that the Superior should serve for a fixed term of six years.

Abbey The monastery where monks live and the convent where nuns live.

Annals The daily record of the activities of a convent.

Archbishop An archbishop administers an archdiocese, which is a really large diocese. In Ireland there are four archdioceses: Armagh, Cashel, Dublin and Tuam.

Benedict St Benedict lived in sixth-century Italy (c.480–547). He founded twelve monasteries of twelve monks each. The envy of the local clergy led him to abandon that settlement and, with some disciples, he founded Monte Cassino, about eighty miles south of Rome. The Rule of St Benedict is followed by all monks and nuns who call themselves Benedictines.

Bishop A bishop oversees a diocese, which is a collection of local parishes.

Cellarer The person in a monastery responsible for provisioning and catering.

Chantress The Chantress directs the choir and composes sacred music. She has charge of the teaching of singing in the convent.

Choir sisters	Nuns who are under obligation to attend all choir offices, as contrasted with lay sisters, who, though living under rule, attend only certain services. This distinction was removed after the Second Vatican Council (1962–5).
Cloister	An enclosed part of a convent or monastery, which is free from entry by outsiders.
Convent	A community of nuns; also, the building in which they live.
Divine Office	Book of prayer, comprising psalms, hymns and lessons, recited or sung daily in choir by professed religious; it is composed of eight hours (Matins, Lauds, Prime, Terce, Sext, None, Vespers, Compline).
Enclosure	Rule of cloistered orders of nuns by which they live always within the convent and do not go into the outside world, except in special cases provided for by Canon Law.
Habit	Distinctive clothing worn by members of a religious order.
Infirmarian	The Infirmarian is trained to serve as pharmacist and physician to the convent.
Lay sisters	Members of a religious institute of women who are not bound by choir duty. Their role is to serve the physical and temporal needs of the community. The distinction between lay sisters and choir sisters was removed after the Second Vatican Council (1962–5).
Lectio divina	Literally 'divine reading', *lectio divina* is an ancient way of reading and praying with the Bible. It has a place of honour in monastic life generally and especially among the practices of Benedictine life.

Novice	Person formally received into a religious community to serve a period of formation that determines fitness for profession.
Novitiate	Term used to refer to both the building in which novices live separated from the professed religious and the time of probation spent under the direction of a Mistress of Novices before a novice is admitted to religious profession.
Nun	Female member of a religious order who has taken solemn vows. The term refers to women religious who have entered contemplative life. Though distinct from 'Sister', the terms are now commonly used interchangeably.
Postulant	Candidate for admission to a religious community who serves a probationary period before being admitted to the novitiate.
Prioress	After her election, the Abbess appoints a Prioress as her deputy.
Profession	Act of embracing religious life, generally by taking vows of Poverty, Chastity and Obedience according to the Rule of the religious order. Benedictines take vows of Stability, Conversion of Manners and Obedience.
Reception	Ceremony, sometimes referred to as Clothing Ceremony, at which a postulant is officially received into a religious order as a novice.
VLA	Venerable Lady Abbess, historical title of the Superior of a Benedictine community of nuns.

'Let nothing be preferred to the work of God.'

St Benedict (AD 480–547)

CHAPTER ONE

THE IRISH DAMES OF YPRES

Benedictine Nuns and their Convents

In the twentieth century, when they settled in Kylemore, the Irish Dames of Ypres would be influenced in many ways by their distinctly 'Irish' surroundings in Connemara. They flourished even as Ireland secured her independence from Britain and the Irish Free State was formed. But at its moment of foundation, almost two hundred and fifty years earlier, their Ypres monastery was a centre of piety founded 'to relieve the spiritual distress of the English Catholic communities'.[1] Where did the Ypres foundation originate? It belongs to the history of English Benedictine houses exiled from England in the seventeenth century. To understand how they came into existence, it is necessary to look at the origins of Benedictine convents.[2]

St Benedict of Nursia founded twelve monasteries in the vicinity of Subiaco, Italy, in the early decades of the sixth century. In 530, he founded the great Benedictine monastery of Monte Cassino, which lies on a hilltop between Rome and Naples. It would appear that St Benedict never had in mind to found a religious order, rather each Benedictine monastery was to be autonomous and under the guidance of an abbot. Benedict's sister, St Scholastica, was the first Benedictine nun, so Benedictine monasticism has had monks and nuns from when it first began. While the Irish Benedictines at Kylemore Abbey trace their history to the first monasteries of St Benedict, they are directly connected to the English Benedictine houses of the seventh century.

The first English Benedictine convent was the Abbey of Folkestone, founded in AD 630. At around this time, convents were being founded in England for daughters of the nobility. There were many nuns of royal blood, including princesses and queens. Barking Abbey had, as abbesses, three queens and two princesses: Queen Edelthryd was abbess of Ely and her sister, Sexburga, succeeded her in office.[3] Convents were part of the religious life of the people; and abbesses were consulted on many issues, including public disputes. They participated in ecclesiastical meetings and they were respected as wise women. Anglo-Saxon convents were often situated close to monasteries for monks. In some instances, the centralised government of both communities was under the authority of the abbess.[4] The seventh century also saw a large number of convents being founded in Gaul and many of these bound themselves to the Rule of St Benedict. In the centuries that followed, Benedictine convents were founded in countries including France, Italy, Germany, Spain, Portugal, Poland, Hungary and Denmark. By the year 1200, 'all the countries of Western Christendom had convents according to the Rule of St Benedict'.[5]

In the Early Middle Ages, the legal position of Benedictine convents varied, depending on their circumstances. They were under the supervision of the bishop in whose diocese they were located and the bishop consecrated the abbess and the nuns, and had the right to make visitation of the convent. Many convents also recognised the authority of an abbot. Additionally, if a convent was established by a king or emperor, it was a royal or imperial convent and had royal protection. Alongside imperial or royal convents, there was a multitude of 'dependent convents', some of which were under the direction of an elected abbess. As a mark of distinction, the abbess of the Middle Ages carried a staff. Other officials in the convent included the chantress, who directed the choir and composed music; the infirmarian, who was trained to serve as pharmacist and physician to the convent, and the teachers, who gave lessons in Latin, reading, writing, music and needlework. Following the Rule of St Benedict, the nuns performed domestic work and managed their bakery and garden. They accepted lay sisters to do domestic work, though the numbers of lay Benedictines remained small until the eighteenth century. Communities lived on the produce from their farms and they rented land and vineyards to servants and tenants, to raise income.

Religious life for nuns centred on the performance of choir service. By the Middle Ages, the nuns' choir was located in a gallery within the church, or in an upper storey of the church, while the vault of the church often served as a tomb. Nuns spent much time walking and praying in the cloisters and reading was done in niches along the cloister. There was also a scriptorium for the copyists and scribes. Some nuns were particularly known for their scholarship and theological training, such as St Hildegard of Bingen and Elizabeth of Schönau.[6] The Benedictine house was a place where the word of God was read and heard, as well as put into practice. The emphasis on 'listening' to the scriptures, through the Benedictine practice of *lectio divina*, was – and still is – central to Benedictine monasticism.[7]

Lady Mary Percy and the Benedictine Foundation at Ypres

The thirteenth century saw a decline in Benedictinism, which has been linked to economic changes. Convents were generally small and relied on barter and their own industry in order to survive. Poor harvests, crop failures, bad management and internal disputes all served to weaken the fabric of monastic life. Convents were also made weak through the practice of having to accept noblewomen who had no

serious commitment to religious life. In the fourteenth and fifteenth centuries, the number of nuns in convents fell. In France and England, the Black Plague and the Hundred Years' War contributed to the demise of many convents. When the Protestant Reformation brought about the complete suppression of the English monasteries, nuns were forced to either abandon religious life or flee to continental Europe. By 1539, there was no longer 'a single convent in England'.[8] However, this was not the end of the English convents; in the century that followed, the English convents in exile joined other communities on the Continent and new convents were founded. The first post-Reformation community of English Benedictines to be established on the Continent was the monastery of the Glorious Assumption of Our Lady, founded by Lady Mary Percy in Brussels in 1598.[9]

The foundation in Brussels, which was made by Lady Mary Percy, was intended for English women who wanted to follow the Benedictine way of life. Until its foundation, such women had 'no choice but to join existing communities on the Continent', even though they often did not speak their language.[10] The Brussels foundation had the support of missionaries in England, who recruited postulants, and it flourished. As the congregation expanded, it became clear that filiations, or daughter houses, were needed to help accommodate the growing community. A convent was established in Cambray (Cambrai) in 1623 and another was founded in Ghent in 1624.[11] In turn, the convent at Ghent became the mother house to four Benedictine houses: Boulogne (1652), Pontoise (1658), Dunkirk (1662) and finally Ypres (1665).[12]

The Ghent convent, known as the Abbey of the Immaculate Conception of Our Blessed Lady, was founded by a group of nuns from the Brussels convent, under the spiritual guidance of Jesuit confessors.

Facing page: Lady Mary Percy, foundress of the monastery of the Glorious Assumption of Our Lady, Brussels (1598).

In 1665, a daughter house of the Ghent community was founded at Ypres, when the Bishop of Ypres, Martin de Praets, invited them into his diocese. The bishop was familiar with the work of the Benedictines in Ghent and, wanting a similar foundation for Ypres, he made a special request that Dame Marina Beaumont be appointed to lead the new foundation on account of her 'fluency in languages'.[13] In 1665, Dame Marina Beaumont became the first lady abbess of the Benedictines in Ypres and nuns from the communities in both Ghent and Dunkirk were chosen to join her.[14] The Ypres monastery, known as Gratia Dei, was 'the last foundation of English Benedictine nuns in exile'.[15]

Bishop de Praets had acquired temporary premises to serve as a convent and had promised to support the building of a more permanent abbey. However, when he died within a year of the arrival of the nuns, the future of the community was uncertain. In the preceding years, the situation in Ypres had been difficult as the nuns were unable to expand their community. Although a number of nuns had been sent from the Benedictine communities in Ghent, Pontoise and Dunkirk, to help with the foundation, none remained long.[16] Until 1681, the only two constants in the Ypres community were Abbess Beaumont and Dame Flavia Carey.[17] In 1671, the little community had to give up their house but a new abbey was secured in Rue St Jacques. It would serve as home to the Ypres community for the next 243 years.

To expand the community, Abbess Beaumont entered into negotiation with the Abbess of Pontoise, Anne Neville. Abbess Beaumont had hoped that if she surrendered the Ypres foundation to the community in Pontoise, 'Ypres would be supplied by subjects from them and so by consequence to be by consent of all for future times to be dependant [sic] on that of Pontoise.'[18] No agreement was reached and Abbess Beaumont subsequently approached the Paris community for help in the matter.[19] According to Abbess Neville, in 1681, 'My Lady Marina [Beaumont] made conditions with the Benedictine Dames at Paris and took two of theirs away with her …

[and] by the favour of friends my Lady Marina procured some good charities and a yearly pension from the King of France, so she and her company returned home with much joy.'[20]

The Irish Dames of Ypres

Encouraged by support from the community in Paris, the Dames of Ypres became more optimistic for the future of their foundation. However, this period of tranquillity was short-lived. In 1682, Abbess Beaumont died and confusion around the affiliation of the house emerged. According to the Ypres Annals:

> The Nuns of Ypres, discontented with the translation of their house, informed the Community of Gent of Lady Beaumont's transaction. Lady Knatchbull, then Abbess of Gent, engaged Lady Caryl, Abbess of Dunkirk, to go to Ypres in order to keep the house for the Congregation, to take with her sufficient subjects to elect an Abbess for a Community of Irish; as she always intended that the house of Ypres should serve for that nation …[21]

The Dames from Paris were forced to relinquish their claims on Ypres and they returned to their Mother House. The annals record:

> As soon as Lady Caryl [Abbess of Dunkirk] received the account of Lady Beaumont's death (which happened on 27 August 1682), she came to Ypres, with four of her religious, two of whom being Irish, she desired they should join the Nuns of Ypres house and elect an Abbess; that the person elected was to be chosen in quality of the first Abbess of an Irish Community …[22]

The Abbess of Ghent, Abbess Knatchbull, directed that the Benedictine filiations of Ghent send some of their professed Irish-born religious to complete the foundation in Ypres. Among the first Irish Dames of Ypres were Dame Ursula Butler (Ghent); Dame Mary Joseph O'Bryan (Dunkirk) and Dame Mary Joseph Butler (Pontoise).[23] On 19 November 1682, Dame Flavia Carey was appointed Lady Abbess of the Irish Benedictine foundation in Ypres, henceforth 'dedicated to the Immaculate Conception of the Blessed Virgin, under the title of Gratia Dei'.[24] From this time, the community in Ypres became known as *De Iersche Damen* (the Irish Dames).

Two Dublin Foundations, 1687–9

Finally established in Ypres, the pioneering nuns set about securing the future of their foundation. There were several expeditions to Ireland, to gather pupils for their school and postulants for their novitiate. In 1684, Dame Joseph Ryan returned from one such expedition with six young girls for the school and two postulants and the future must have looked promising.[25] The impact of penal laws on Irish Catholics had caused those who were wealthy to send their daughters abroad for their education. Dame Joseph Ryan knew that the school could attract more young Irish women and she embarked on another journey, questing for vocations in Ireland.[26] However, while she was away, the community suffered a setback when the Lady Abbess, Dame Flavia Carey, died. There were only three choir nuns in the community at the time and the Ypres nuns were required to obtain assistance from the other Benedictine houses in order to appoint a successor.[27] Dame Mary Joseph Butler was subsequently elected Lady Abbess, a position which she retained until her death in 1723.[28]

Meanwhile, during her travels in Ireland, Dame Ryan learned of the election and was displeased. She may have expected the election to be postponed until her return or she may simply have not supported Dame

Portrait of King James II.

Butler's appointment. In any case, Dame Ryan decided not to return to Ypres. Instead, she petitioned the Archbishop of Dublin, Dr Patrick Russell, for permission to establish a foundation in the city. The recent succession of the Catholic King James II to the throne would have suggested to Dame Ryan that the time was perfect for the establishment of a Benedictine house in Ireland.[29] At the time, Benedictine foundations were autonomous and independent, subject only to the jurisdiction of the local bishop. Dame Ryan had made an earlier attempt to establish an Irish foundation in Dunkirk and still harboured a desire to establish her own monastery. Following the granting of formal approval from Bishop Russell, Dame Ryan obtained premises in Channel Row and began her Benedictine foundation in 1687.[30] Unsurprisingly, back in Ypres, Lady Abbess Butler was extremely critical of Dame Ryan's actions and the subsequent loss of potential students and postulants. The situation undoubtedly became even more difficult when, in 1687, Lady Abbess Butler was invited to establish another foundation in Dublin.

In 1685, James II became King of England and Ireland, following the death of his brother, Charles II. The succession of James II was widely welcomed by Catholics in Ireland and England, including the Benedictines. Indeed Abbess Knatchbull, at Ghent, carried on a correspondence with both James II and his wife, Mary of Modena.[31] She was just one of many nuns involved in Jacobite support, at a time when 'religious women's spiritual patronage was highly sought after at the English court'.[32] The nuns were confident of the king's support following his accession, and – despite the brevity of his reign – they were not disappointed: the Catholic king directed the lord lieutenant, the Duke of Tyrconnell, to invite the Irish Dames of Ypres to come to Dublin.[33]

Suitable premises were found on Great Ship Street and were to be given to the community rent and tax free, and James II promised £100 a year for the maintenance of the nuns and the convent.[34] Before the nuns left Ypres, Tyrconnell had written to the Grand Vicars of Ypres requesting that the abbey be retained there in case the foundation in Dublin did not succeed.[35] Because the numbers in the community in Ypres were still small, four nuns from Pontoise were selected to lead

Facing page: Portrait of Lady Abbess Mary Joseph Butler, 3rd Abbess of Ypres (1686–1723).

the foundation: Dame Margaret Markham, Dame Mary Lawson, Dame Anne Neville and Dame Susan Fletcher.[36] They arrived in Dublin in late September 1687 and took possession of the little convent in Great Ship Street which had been acquired for them by Tyrconnell.[37] In 1689, they were joined by the Irish Dames from Ypres: Lady Abbess Butler and Dames Barbara Philpott and Placida Holmes.[38]

The convent and school in Great Ship Street had not been in operation for more than two years when political and social unrest forced the nuns to abandon their mission. Although the Duke of Ormonde, a distant relation of Lady Abbess Butler, had promised protection of

Abbaye des Bénédictines Irlandaises, Ypres (Lithograph, Bruges).

the Irish Benedictines, Lady Abbess Butler was determined that they should return to Ypres.[39] Acceding to his cousin's wishes, the Duke of Ormonde obtained safe passage for the nuns from Great Ship Street and they returned to Ypres on 23 July 1690.[40] Around the same time, Dame Ryan's convent in Channel Row was also forced to close by the Williamite forces. While Lady Abbess Butler returned to the convent in Ypres to try to rebuild the Benedictine foundation there, Dame Ryan remained in Ireland hopeful that circumstances would change. However, she eventually returned to Dunkirk where she died on 7 September 1719 at the age of ninety-two.[41]

Letter of permission to Dame Mary Joseph Butler to leave Ypres for Dublin (1688).

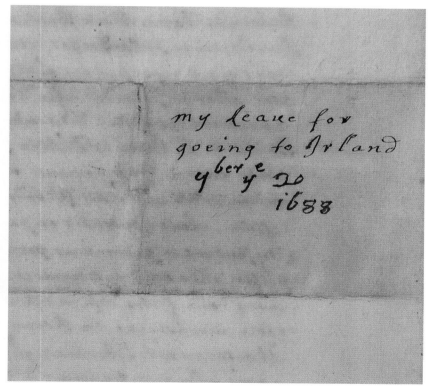

Vicaires generaux de L'Euesché
d'Ipre vacant. A bons Ceux qui cespresentes
Lettres voiront salut. scauoir faisons que la
Reuerende Dame Marie Butler Abbesse des
Benedictines Irlandoises establies a Ipre
nous ajant representée qu'elle estoit requise
pour aller en Irlande afin d'establir Vn
monastere des filles dudit ordre de sainct
Benoit en La Ville de Dublein suppliant pour
auoir nostre consentement, et nos Lettres
obedientialles; Voulans seconder son pieux
dessein, auons Consentis et permis, Commes
Consentons et permettons par Ceste qu'elle
puisse aller en Engleterre et en Irlande
auec q deux filles de sa maison pour establir
Ledit monastere, La Recommandans a
Monseigneur L'Archeuecque de Dublein, et
à tous autres, et les prians de la fauorizer
pour executer ses bons et pieux desseins. En
foy de quoy auons fait signer ceste par nostre
secretaire, et seller de nostre seel. faict à
Ipre le 20.e Septembre 1688.

Par ordonnance de Messieurs
les Vicaires generaux

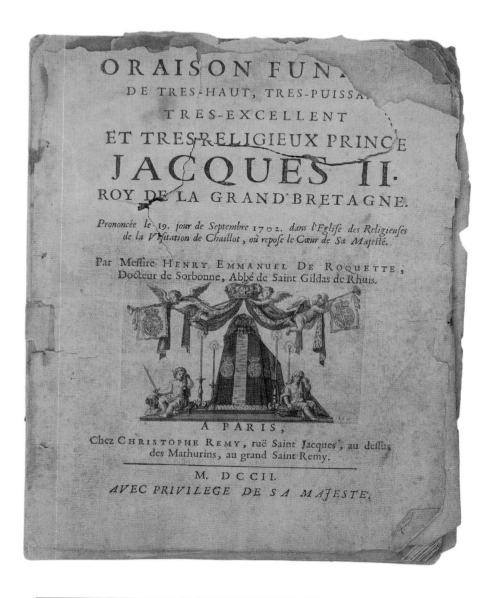

ORAISON FUN...
DE TRES-HAUT, TRES-PUISSA...
TRES-EXCELLENT
ET TRES-RELIGIEUX PRINCE
JACQUES II.
ROY DE LA GRAND'BRETAGNE.

Prononcée le 19. jour de Septembre 1702. dans l'Eglise des Religieuses
de la Visitation de Chaillot, où repose le Cœur de Sa Majesté.

Par Messire HENRY EMMANUEL DE ROQUETTE,
Docteur de Sorbonne, Abbé de Saint Gildas de Rhuis.

A PARIS,
Chez CHRISTOPHE REMY, ruë Saint Jacques', au dessus
des Mathurins, au grand Saint Remy.

M. DCCII.
AVEC PRIVILEGE DE SA MAJESTE.

Above: Funeral Oration of King James II (1702).

Facing page: Letter of permission to Dame Mary Joseph Butler to leave Ypres for Dublin (1688).

15

The Irish Dames of Ypres, 1690–1914

On returning to Ypres in 1690, Abbess Butler was faced with the difficult challenge of trying to rebuild the Irish foundation there. According to the annals of the Benedictine convent in Ypres:

> After a long and dangerous voyage both by sea and land they at length arrived at Ypres, and entered their old house, where Lady Butler led a most solitary life … For five years she [was] alone with four lay sisters, and in … extreme poverty … resisting the solicitations of her family, and even the Bishops, to sell the house and live at her ease wherever she chose; but her heroic soul, confiding in Providence, would not abandon the work of God …[42]

In 1695, four young women were admitted to the convent in Ypres as novices. However, only two, Dame Arthur and Dame Josepha O'Connor, were professed in December 1700. According to the annals, 'Notwithstanding her want of subjects she had the resolution to dismiss the other two, not finding them endowed with the spirit of their state.'[43] This dismissal is even more surprising when it seems that the 'Queen of England had promised to provide for their maintenance'.[44] Indeed, Mary of Modena had a strong devotion to the Irish Dames of Ypres. Other benefactors of the period included Pope Innocent XII and the King of France.[45]

Over the next couple of decades, the little community in Ypres gradually grew and its future was more secure by the time Lady Abbess Butler died on 22 December 1723. For the next 117 years, the position of abbess was held by Irish-born nuns: Lady Abbess Butler was succeeded

Facing page: Lady Abbess Bernard Lynch, 8th Abbess of Ypres (1799–1830).

Above: Benedictine Abbey of Ypres (n.d.).

Facing page: Nun walking in the gardens at Benedictine Abbey of Ypres (n.d.).

Above: Two nuns in corridor at Benedictine Abbey of Ypres (n.d.).

Facing page, from top:

Nun kneeling in Choir at Benedictine Abbey of Ypres (n.d.).

Nun walking in the grounds of Benedictine Abbey of Ypres (n.d.).

by Lady Abbess Xaveria Arthur (1723–43); Lady Abbess Magdalen Mandeville (1743–60); Lady Abbess Bernard Dalton (1760–83); Lady Abbess Scholastica Lynch (1783–99); Lady Abbess Bernard Lynch (1799–1830); and Lady Abbess Benedict Byrne (1830–40).[46]

The Ypres convent developed a reputation for education and ran a successful boarding school. Most of the young girls sent to board there would have been the daughters of members of the English and Irish Catholic upper ranks, who were deprived of Catholic schooling at home. In part because of its series of Irish-born abbesses, Ypres became known as a convent that attracted Irish families. For example, there is some possibility that Nano Nagle, who would later found the Sisters of the Presentation of the Blessed Virgin Mary (PBVM), was sent from Cork to be educated in Ypres in the early eighteenth century.[47] The Ypres community spoke and taught through English, making the school well suited to Irish families like the Nagles. The rate at which Irish girls were sent to Ypres slowed from the start of the nineteenth century, however. At that point, with the relaxation of relevant penal laws, convents were again being established in Ireland. Orders such as the Ursulines (OSU) and the Loretos (IBVM) were opening boarding schools for the daughters of the Catholic elite in Cork and Dublin. Loss of income as a result of the decrease in Irish pupils was felt in Ypres: in 1784, Lady Abbess Lynch wrote several times to Teresa Mulally in Dublin, asking Mulally to 'procure an encrase in pensionners' for the Ypres school.[48]

In 1840, Lady Abbess Byrne was succeeded by an English-born Dame, Lady Abbess Elizabeth Jarrett (1840–88), thus bringing to an end the era of Irish Abbesses at the Benedictine Abbey in Ypres.[49] For a period under Dame Jarrett's term as Abbess, there were no Irish-born Dames living in the community. In 1854, Dame Joseph Fletcher arrived in Ypres and 'united the community again to "old Ireland"'.[50] Lady Abbess Jarrett died in September 1888 and was succeeded by Dame Scholastica Bergé (1890–1916).[51] Under Lady Abbess Bergé, a 'stream of vocations … [began] to flow again' and 'the daughters of Erin [found] their way

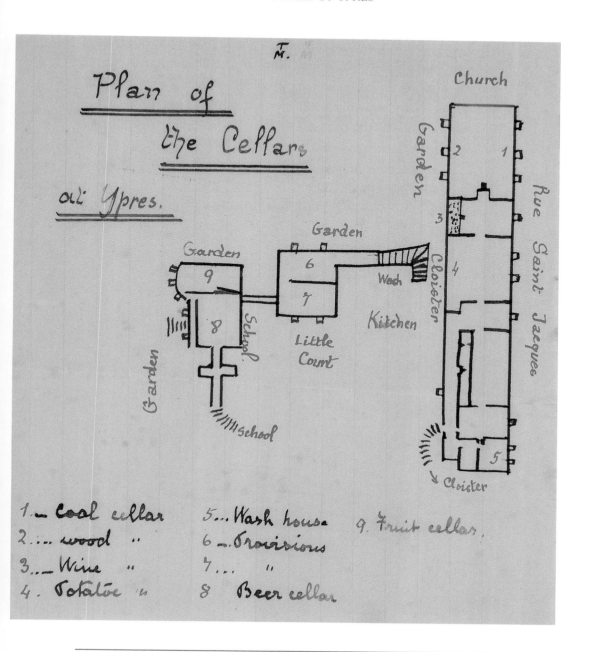

Cellar plan, Benedictine Abbey of Ypres (n.d.).

once more to the Convent of the Irish Dames, the only Benedictine convent which Irishwomen can call their own'.[52] In the absence of any records from the Ypres monastery, it is impossible to say exactly who these Irishwomen were; however, it is reasonable to suggest that they were young women who had been educated by teaching sisters at some of the many hundred convent schools that spread across Ireland in the mid-nineteenth century.[53] With increasing vocations, a period of stability and growth followed.

All of this was shattered when, in July 1914, the First World War broke out.

Above: Pupils dressed for pageant at the Benedictine Abbey of Ypres (n.d.).
Overleaf: Benedictine Abbey of Ypres after the bombing in 1914.

From left to right:
Sr Dorothy Ryan, Sr Noreen Gallagher, Sr Genevieve Harrington,
Mother Máire Hickey, Sr Aidan Ryan, Sr Magdalena FitzGibbon,
Sr Marie Genevieve Mukamana, Sr Karol O'Connell, Sr Mary Jiao

PAX

TURN HANDLE AND
PUSH

Above, from left to right:
Sr Noreen Gallagher,
Sr Aidan Ryan, Sr Karol
O'Connell, Sr Marie
Genevieve Mukamana,
Mother Máire Hickey,
Sr Genevieve Harrington,
Sr Magdalena FitzGibbon,
Sr Dorothy Ryan,
Sr Mary Jiao

'… selfhood begins in the walking away
And love is proved in the letting go.'

Cecil Day-Lewis (1904–72)

CHAPTER TWO

THE JOURNEY TOWARDS KYLEMORE,
1914–1920

The First Battle of Ypres

On 28 July 1914, one month to the day after Archduke Franz Ferdinand of Austria and his wife were killed by a Serbian nationalist in Sarajevo, Austria-Hungary declared war on Serbia. A few days later, Germany declared war on Russia and Britain declared war on Germany. After advancing relatively quickly through Belgium and eastern France during the first weeks of the war, the Germans suffered defeat in September in the Battle of the Marne. In that month, all German nationals were expelled from Belgium.[1] In the Benedictine Abbey in Ypres, four members of the community were German. They had to leave the country immediately, travelling first from Ypres to Bruges; the Bishop assisted their passage from there to Holland.[2] The remaining fifteen nuns (fourteen professed and one novice) had expected that their German sisters would return within a few weeks but, on 7 October, a German aeroplane passed over the town and shortly afterwards, at about 1.30 p.m., everyone was startled by the sound of firing close by. Dame Columban Plomer wrote: 'In the Monastery, it was the spiritual-reading hour, so we were not able to communicate our fears; but, instead of receding, the sound came nearer, till, at 2 o'clock, the shots from the guns literally made the house shake.'[3] The nuns did not know what was happening until 'Reverend Mother Prioress announced … [that] the Germans were in the town.'[4]

The strategy of both sides in the war after that was to secure the ports on the English Channel, beginning what became known as the 'Race to the Sea'. German forces launched a major offensive that aimed to push forward to the Channel ports of Dunkirk and Calais. Ypres, located on the northeast corner of Belgium bordering France, was in an extremely important position strategically, as it was effectively the fortress blocking their route. To achieve their objectives, it was necessary for Germany to take Ypres; for the Entente it was essential to ensure that they failed. This resulted in the First Battle of Ypres, which lasted until late November, and was described as 'the centre of the most terrible fighting in the War'.[5]

By the end of October, it had become apparent that the fighting was not going to end as soon as had at first been widely believed. The burgomaster sent round word that from henceforward until further orders, no strong lights should be visible from outside the monastery and no bells should be rung from six in the evening until the following day. Consequently, when night fell, the monastery remained in darkness, each nun contenting herself with the minimum of light. A few strokes of a little handbell summoned the community to hours of regular observance, instead of the familiar sound of the belfry-bell, which had, for two and a half centuries, rung out each succeeding hour. Inside the monastery, the nuns 'were no longer able to say the office in the choir, as on one side the windows looked on the street, and on the other to the garden, the light being thus clearly visible from the ramparts'.[6] Instead, they 'said compline and matins, first in the workroom and afterwards in the chapter-house, placing a double set of curtains on the windows to prevent the least little glimmer of light from being seen from the outside'.[7]

The Irish Dames Leave Ypres

Many of the inhabitants of the town were forced to leave as 'dwelling places and public buildings had been destroyed'.[8] It was therefore decided that, in case of emergency, each nun should prepare a parcel of what was most necessary, 'lest the worst should come, and [they] should be obliged to fly'.[9] At first, it was felt that only their Abbess, Dame Bergé, should be removed and sent to Poperinge for her safety. She left the enclosure reluctantly: she had not stepped outside the Abbey in sixty years. Some days later, the nuns 'managed to gather some things, which were needed, and to get out of the town just as the guns were beginning again'.[10] Prioress Ostyn, with the last of the Irish Dames of Ypres, left the Abbey and walked the nine miles to Poperinge, where they were given shelter by a community of La Sainte Union nuns. For two weeks they stayed in Poperinge until they secured transport to Boulogne.

On the last day of October, German cavalry units had begun a more concentrated attack. Over the next three weeks, the fighting was chaotic, with casualty figures on both sides mounting as the weather grew cold and blustery. On 22 November, amid high winds and blizzards, fighting was suspended completely and the First Battle of Ypres came to an end. Both sides suffered heavy losses. Germany lost approximately 130,000 men compared with Entente losses of around 100,000 soldiers. Casualties amongst the British Expeditionary Force effectively destroyed Britain's highly trained pre-war army.[11] On that same day, the nuns left Boulogne and sailed for England. After a short stay in London, they made their way to the Benedictine Abbey in Oulton, Staffordshire, in response to a pressing invitation from the Abbess. This generous gesture of hospitality reflected the longstanding relationship between these two great abbeys.

The Ypres Benedictines remained at Oulton for six months. However, they knew this was a temporary home for them and that they would have to find a more permanent one. The Mother Prioress hoped to revisit Ypres in order to recover some valuables.[12] However, that trip did not happen as the nuns failed to get passports for Belgium. They travelled from Oulton to Highfield House, in Golders Green, London, where they were given hospitality by the Daughters of Wisdom for a further nine months. This community had belonged to the convent of La Sagesse, which had been suppressed and the nuns expelled by the French government a decade earlier. Having settled in London, the Daughters of Wisdom were now in charge of Highfield House, where they were looking after Belgian refugees. To the Benedictines, Highfield House seemed 'large and commodious … [with] a little chapel in the grounds'.[13] Later, the nuns 'learned that it was really Protestant and only blessed and made fit for our use since the outbreak of the war'.[14] When they said goodbye to the Lady Abbess and all the community at Oulton, they were 'loaded with so many presents that they were obliged to [take] a small trunk to put them in!'[15]

All the while, they still hoped to return to Ypres. To this end, a national fund was set up 'with the support of John Redmond and others, to help the nuns during their stay in England and to finance any future restoration work at Ypres'.[16] However, the war continued with no signs of abating and all hopes of returning to Ypres began to diminish. An account from Henry V. Gill SJ, who was Catholic chaplain to the 2nd Royal Irish Rifles in France from November 1914, provides some insight into the fate of the Benedictine Abbey at Ypres during the First World War. In January 1915, Gill made his first visit to Ypres two months after the Dames had left the convent:

> At this time the convent was by no means a complete wreck. The upper rooms appeared to be intact. They were locked up and were filled with the nuns' belongings. Notices in French were attached to the doors, signed by military authorities, forbidding anyone to enter.[17]

In May 1915, Gill visited Ypres for the second time. Continuous gas attacks and incendiary shells had reduced Ypres to 'a city of the dead'.[18] The Benedictine convent did not escape the destruction; it was 'completely gutted by fire. All the inner rooms and flooring [were] burnt away. The walls still remained, but nothing else. With a sad exception, the cellars had escaped.'[19]

Meanwhile, the Dames in England had not left the war behind. The nuns recalled:

> September 8th: At 10 o'clock last night just as we had got into bed, we were startled by a terrific bang-bang-clack. A zepplin a zepplin! [sic] The first bang was followed by a second still louder and nearer. It seemed to be actually on the house. By this time everyone was wide awake and in the corridor in night attire. We all went down to the garden and we were witness of a really interesting but awful sight. The search lights were playing in the sky, at a certain moment they all concentrated in one particular spot, that part of the sky was all a glow … shots were fired but none of them struck the zepplin [sic] though one went very near … our eyes were fixed on it and our hearts stood still as we saw that dreadful thing pass quite over our house. It dipped and disappeared in the dark, after that our attention was attracted by the peculiar colour of a certain part of the sky … About 12.30 everything seemed calm and we went off to bed after having said a prayer for protection. We heard some more bombs dropping between 1 and 2 o'clock but they were further off in the city. Sept 9th: After Mass we went down to see the damage done by the bomb … the kitchen windows were all broken … [the bomb] was found in a garden a few yards from us, the hole was big enough to contain a horse and cart. There was a great raid through London about 60 persons killed, 7 here at Golder's Green …[20]

The Benedictine Community, Merton House, Macmine, County Wexford (*c.*1916–18).

Arrival in Ireland

It is not clear if the Irish Dames of Ypres were aware at this time of the complete and utter destruction of their abbey. In any event, they were visited at Highfield by the Lord Abbot Marmion OSB, who had recently procured a property at Edermine in County Wexford, near Enniscorthy, for his monks in exile from Maredsous. He suggested that Mother Prioress should travel to Ireland to view a possible property for the establishment of a monastery for their nuns and she agreed to this proposal. On her journey to Ireland she was accompanied by Dame Teresa Howard who recorded the trip in a diary. The nuns took the train from Euston and the boat to Kingstown (Dún Laoghaire), followed by another train to Enniscorthy. There a pony and trap had been sent to take them to see the Curtis family and visit Merton House, which was for sale. Dame Teresa recorded:

> One place upon a height showed such a beautiful view that we all declared a monastery must be built there in future years, and we even called it St Bride's Abbey. In the afternoon we drove to Merton with Fr Prior and Bridget [Curtis] and visited the house and grounds; we found the former in a somewhat dilapidated state, no one having lived in it for the last two years, the garden also was neglected and looked like a wilderness, but the grounds around, the avenues, the alleys, and the magnificent view on the Slaney river were beyond description. Immediately we made up our minds that, if God willed it, Merton House was to become our new Ypres Abbey and from that moment all our prayers and our efforts were devoted to that one object.[21]

The Curtis family became good friends to the nuns, who spent their evenings in the kitchen where Mrs Curtis, whom they named Mother General, supplied warm hospitality and even sang and danced for them. When they were leaving, she gave them her recipe book.[22] The nuns, in turn, left a lasting impression on the Curtis family, one member of whom became the first Benedictine postulant in Ireland.

The nuns went on to Macmine Castle to visit Captain and Mrs Corballis, who would be their neighbours. They were offered hospitality there until their offer on Merton House was accepted. In February 1916, they secured the lease on Merton House, Macmine, 'a plain square building with 40 acres of land and good garden'.[23] An appeal for funds to the Irish people had a generous response and helped the community to settle there and set to work straight away to establish the first Benedictine monastery in Ireland since the Reformation.

Although the First World War was not waged on Irish soil, the Easter Rising, within two months of their arrival, brought back unhappy memories of Ypres and of London. A pencilled note records the impact of the hostilities on the newly established monastery: '27th [April] Edermine bridge blown up. Priest came down Slaney in boat for Mass.' And two days later, when there was a danger that the monastery would be cut off without food: '29th [April] Provisions by boat from Wexford.'[24] The political situation nationally also had a financial impact:

It had been the intention of our benefactors to issue a fresh appeal for funds to equip the house as soon as the purchase price £1059 had been reached; but the Easter Rising brought Mr R[edmond]'s influence to an end and we thus found ourselves without even the necessaries. The Refugee Committee granted us 10/- a week per head as long as War lasted. We farmed the land, working in the fields ourselves, and in September the same year a couple of girls were entrusted to our care for Education. Thereupon our school began and before the end of the year they had been joined by several others.[25]

In November 1916, Lady Abbess Scholastica Bergé died. Her life in religion had included serving in many roles at the Abbey at Ypres,

including Mistress in the school, Assistant Infirmarian, Assistant Cellarer, Cellarer and Prioress. The 11th Abbess, Dame Scholastica, had brought the community through severe trials and had delivered them to their new home in Ireland. In her final years, her frailty had obliged Dame Scholastica to rely heavily on the Prioress, Dame Maura Ostyn, and it was Dame Maura who was elected to succeed her as the 12th Abbess.

Under Lady Abbess Maura Ostyn, the nuns started their new life in County Wexford. Some girls began to look for education and

---

Facing page:

Lady Abbess Maura Ostyn (c.1916–18), 12th Abbess at Macmine Abbey.

Below: Advertisement for the Select Boarding School, Ypres Benedictine Abbey, Macmine, County Wexford (1917).

2 6 OCT 1917

The Irish Nuns of Ypres

The Irish Benedictine Dames of the Royal Abbey of the Immaculate Conception, at Ypres, have, with the cordial approval of His Lordship the Bishop of Ferns, opened a Select Boarding-School, similar to that which they directed for so many years in Belgium.

It is their aim to instil into their Pupils a fervent and solid piety, without which true education cannot exist; together with a judicious notion of personal responsibility—at the same time developing the intellectual and moral qualities.

The Course of Studies comprises all the branches of a superior education, **with the advantages of a continental training.** The system of teaching is adapted to ensure for each Pupil thoroughness in every branch.

Careful attention is given to health, diet and recreation. The neighbourhood is well-known for its beautiful scenery, and the children enjoy a great variety of walks.

For further details and Prospectus apply to—

REV LADY ABBESS, O.S.B.,

Ypres Benedictine Abbey,

Macmine Castle, Co. Wexford.

The Benedictine Community, Macmine Abbey,
County Wexford (November 1920).

were taught informally at first. However, a decision was taken that the community should move to Macmine Castle to live and that the school should be opened in Merton House in September 1917. The nuns recorded:

> We painted and renovated Merton ourselves and in September the school equipped for 30 pupils was full. The school paid well, and the farm provided the greater part of the food for school and community so we were able to keep afloat.[26]

The roll book of 'Pupils educated at Ypres Benedictine Abbey, Merton' lists the first two pupils in 1916 as Miss Marjory Tyler from Dalkey, aged 15, Protestant, and Miss Mary Teresa Cassin from Waterford, aged 14. However, it is the next entry on the roll that shows the close links the nuns maintained with Belgium:

> January 13 1917: Entered our Monastery as boarder Mademoiselle Angèle De Wit, age 16 and her sister Eliza, age 12, refugees from Anvers. They have both to be prepared for their First Communion which they could not make before now on account of the father's opposition; he is a Freemason. Made their First Communion in our chapel on March 26, confirmed by Bishop Codd in our chapel on May 26 1918. Left for Belgium February 19 1919, peace being proclaimed the preceding November.[27]

A number of Belgian pupils came as boarders and left during the Macmine years. The only Irish described as 'day pupils' are four girls – two sets of siblings – the O'Neills and the Doyles. They enrolled in 1917 but left within the year. Miss May Murray from Cork came for a month in the summer of 1917 to learn French. Dame Teresa Howard's diary notes snow storms throughout January and February 1917; in

September and October 1918, they were not spared the 'flu which affected the whole country. Sr Mary Kate Magner, recently professed, and Miss Mary Burke BA, who had come as a secular teacher in September 1917, both died of the 'flu in November 1918.[28]

In all, the Irish Dames of Ypres spent four years in Macmine. They had their hands full, between running the boarding school and managing the farm, so it was a great boon that eleven new entrants joined the community. The clothing ceremony for the first two postulants was reported in the local paper:

THE IRISH NUNS OF YPRES
RELIGIOUS RECEPTION AT MERTON, MACMINE

On Saturday last a religious ceremony of more than ordinary importance took place at Merton, Macmine, the newly-acquired convent of the Benedictine Nuns of Ypres, Belgium, better known as the Irish Nuns of Ypres … It was the first religious ceremony held at Merton since the house was converted into a religious institution … The young postulants who had the happiness of receiving the white veil … were Miss Kate Magner BA Cambridge (in religion Sister Agnes), daughter of Dr and Mrs Magner, Lakelands, Blackrock, Cork, grand-niece of that distinguished Irishman the late Mr A M Sullivan author of *The Story of Ireland*, and niece to Mr T M Healy KC MP. The other young lady is Miss Maggie Josephine Curtis (in religion Sister Mary Benedict), daughter of the late Mr John and Mrs Curtis, Knockduff, Bree, Enniscorthy and sister of Mrs Golden, Tralee.[29]

In 1918, just two years after the arrival of the Benedictines in Ireland, the war in Europe ended and, with the cessation of hostilities, the nuns wondered if they should perhaps return to Ypres. But the destruction of their monastery, as well as the devastation of Belgium generally,

Benedictine nuns doing the laundry at Macmine Abbey,
County Wexford (*c*.1920).

answered that question for them. They made the decision to remain
in Ireland. However, 'it became evident that Macmine Castle – the
residence of the Nuns, and Merton House – the Abbey School, were
quite inadequate from the point of view of healthy accommodation'.[30]
A process of discernment was undertaken, during which the nuns laid
out their options under three headings: 'Inadvisability of remaining at

Macmine; If obliged to remain; If we decide not to remain'.[31] They considered the physical problems with the buildings ('damp, cold, sanitary dangers'); the effect of these on morale ('depressing'); and the drain on their finances caused by 'Rent of castle – expense of heating, lighting, victualling two houses – cooking etc, 10 rooms to be heated at school'. If they were to remain at Macmine Castle, they would have to undertake substantial renovations and if they were to close the school, they would disappoint parents and pupils. Another option was to move to a new location. This was the option that they favoured and they began the process of finding more suitable premises for a monastery and school. It was a difficult process but eventually the Benedictines were pointed in the direction of suitable premises in Connemara:

> Dame Maura Ostyn made numerous journeys only to return to Macmine with the conviction that the future Abbey had yet to be found. On May 3 1919, His Grace Most Rev T Gilmartin, Archbishop of Tuam invited Father Prior to lunch and, during the conversation, spoke of Kylemore as being worth investigating … Lady Abbess and Dame Teresa paid a flying visit to Kylemore to view the place. They were very enthusiastic about the surroundings, and obtained a glimpse of the inside of the Castle, but were obliged to make a hurried departure when the agent in charge of the property became suspicious of their intentions.[32]

By the end of the year 1919, they had episcopal approval from the Archbishop of Tuam to establish a foundation in his diocese. However, the process of securing the property was not easy. Their agent made an approach and the figure quoted was £150,000, at the second £77,000 'and the third and final answer was that the property would not be sold at less than £70,000'.[33] They appointed a different agent who was finally instructed to offer £40,000. Further 'annoyance' occurred which 'caused a delay in so far as the removal from Macmine was not effected till December 2nd'.[34]

Unsurprisingly, in anticipation of its closure, a number of pupils had left the school at Macmine between 1919 and 1920, though some stayed until the very last day, 29 November 1920. A handful of pupils transferred from Wexford to Connemara with the nuns, including Helen Day, who had enrolled in Macmine in 1917.

The emptying of Merton House and Macmine Castle, and the packing of the contents having been completed, the nuns watched as their new lorry made the journey to the railway station laden with their luggage:

> Towards midnight, things grew quieter, as the motor lorries and other vehicles stopped work … How strange it was when midnight came … everything was quiet … we moved about among the remaining objects to see if nothing very special was left … work ceased after midnight, and we prepared for Mass, which Fr Prior said at 1 o'clock. (Friday morning December 3rd 1st Friday Mass was said in thanksgiving for all the graces we received from God during our stay at Macmine.)[35]

By the time Mass was over it was half past two in the morning. When they had prepared a small parcel each, for immediate use on arriving at Kylemore, they went to have a last meal. 'It was Friday but Fr Prior dispensed us from Abstinence, and everyone had meat.'[36] At six o'clock, they left for the station, four or five in each car. Fr Prior went first, in order to help the nuns settle into their carriages; Lady Abbess was the last to leave. The people of Macmine were so sad to see the nuns leave their area that they got up at the dawn to see them off.[37]

It was half past seven when the train pulled out of the station. At Enniscorthy, they were met by Fr Murphy with some gifts for the journey. The long delay in Dublin was made more bearable by the surprise visit of several old pupils and that helped to pass the time. They had expected to have a similar delay in Galway which would necessitate their spending the night there. 'But Providence would have us at our new home on the 1st Friday … somehow or other the Galway to Clifden waited for the Dublin, and so we came straight through from Macmine to Clifden without having to change trains and arrived at Clifden about 11 o'clock.'[38] Although it was close to midnight, Monsignor McAlpine and hundreds of local people were on the platform to welcome them. They piled into the waiting cars, asking their driver to let them know when they were approaching Kylemore. When he shouted, 'There it is!' they peered out into the black Connemara night and 'saw one glow at the foot of a mountain'.[39] This time Lady Abbess was in the first motor car and, as it 'drove up on the terrace, the big bell rang from the tower as the nuns with Lady Abbess entered the house'.[40] Their exhaustion after such a marathon journey can be imagined. Fr Prior, who seems to have been an eminently practical man, instructed them to have a meal and to go to bed. In those days, it was necessary to fast from midnight if one wished to receive Holy Communion in the morning, so he told them that there would be no morning Mass. However, any hope of going to bed was dashed when they found that their beds and bedding had not arrived. So, they simply lay on the floor in various rooms and slept soundly until ten o'clock next morning.

Six years after being exiled from their monastery at Ypres, the Irish Dames had arrived at Kylemore Castle in December 1920. Henceforth, the castle would be known as Kylemore Abbey. On 1 March 1921, the rights and privileges of the Abbey at Ypres were transferred to Kylemore Abbey, making it the first Benedictine monastery established in Ireland since the seventeenth century.

ORA

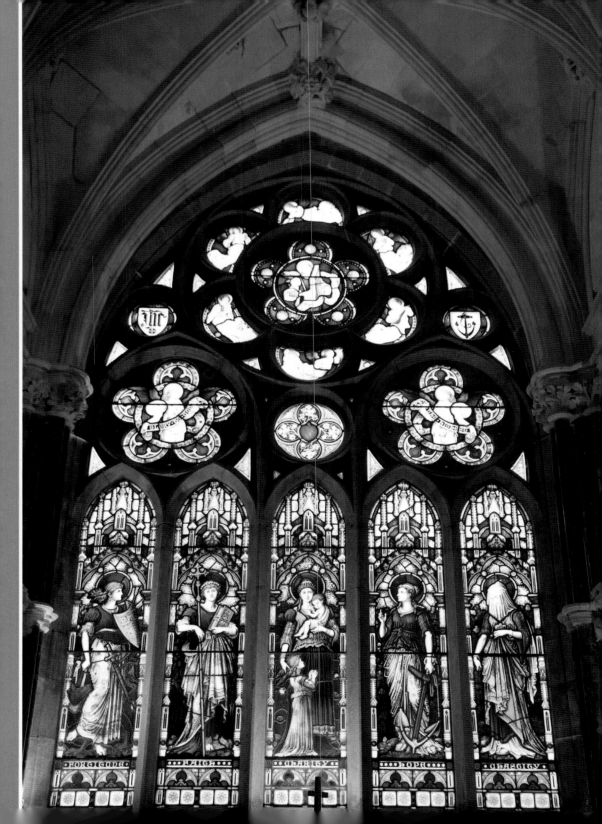

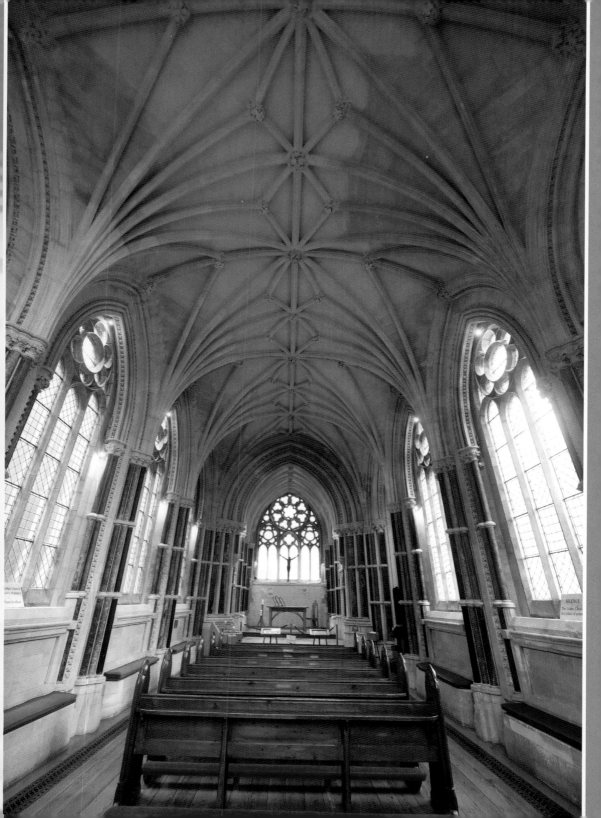

Below, from left
to right:
Sr Aidan Ryan,
Sr Mary Jiao,
Sr Noreen Gallagher,
Sr Magdalena
FitzGibbon,
Sr Karol O'Connell

From left to right:
Sr Aidan Ryan, Sr Mary Jiao, Sr Noreen Gallagher,
Sr Magdalena FitzGibbon, Sr Karol O'Connell, Mother Máire Hickey,
Sr Dorothy Ryan, Sr Marie Genevieve Mukamana, Sr Genevieve Harrington

Sr Mary Jiao

Facing page:
Sr Marie Genevieve Mukamana

Above, from left to right:
Sr Aidan Ryan, Sr Mary Jiao, Sr Genevieve Harrington, Sr Noreen Gallagher,
Mother Máire Hickey, Sr Magdalena FitzGibbon, Sr Dorothy Ryan,
Sr Marie Genevieve Mukamana, Sr Karol O'Connell

'Christian sacrifice is the glad giving up of what is prized, because of a call which is prized even more.'

Dom Hubert van Zeller OSB (1905–84)

CHAPTER THREE

CONNEMARA AND KYLEMORE IN THE NINETEENTH CENTURY

On this occasion the donkey was quite ready to stop, and she surveyed, with a connoisseur's cold eye, the unsurpassable view, while the evening clouds thronged the gap between the steep tree-covered sides of Kylemore on one side, and the stony severities of the Diamond Mountain on the other, and sent changing lights and shadows hurrying over the wide lake, and drove the labouring sketcher of these things almost to madness.[1]

Through Connemara in a Governess Cart (1893)

The Land and the People

The first sight of Kylemore Abbey is one of the most dramatic and memorable of all the tourist sights in Ireland. The castellated and turreted Abbey is nestled under dramatic mountainscape and fronted by a large lake. It has a picture-book appearance that is almost improbable – and its history shows that, indeed, there was nothing organic about the way in which this estate rose from the Connemara landscape. The perfect positioning of the castle, the impact of the vista across Lough Pollacapull and the gardens, orchards and woodlands were all part of the vision and labour of Mitchell Henry, who owned the estate from 1867 to 1902. When the Benedictines arrived in 1920, the area had benefited from Henry's financial investment; but it had also suffered the consequences of a century of famine, emigration, political unrest and poverty.

The imbrication of two narratives – that of the fairy-tale castle and that of impoverished Connemara – had to be absorbed and fully understood by the Benedictines if they were to thrive in west Connaught. As women who belonged to one of the 'English convents in exile', they were now trying to put down permanent roots in Ireland.[2] Somehow, they would have to become landlords on a vast estate, while continuing their commitment to living a simple life of prayer and teaching. Somehow, they would need their neighbours to see them as women of God and not as a group of elite outsiders who were about to determine the future of many local familes whose livelihoods depended on the Kylemore estate. Additionally, Wexford was very different from Connemara and their brief time in Macmine was poor preparation for life in the remote monastery on the side of a lake.

Positioned in one of the farthest points of west Galway, Kylemore in the nineteenth century was part of the Archdiocese of Tuam, which covered a vast geographical area of some 1,400,000 acres and was divided into seven deaneries and fifty-one parishes.[3] The Kylemore estate and lands fell within the parish of Ballynakill, in the Clifden deanery. It was a landscape of mountains, lakes, heather and rock. A few large estates, in Clifden, Renvyle and Letterfrack, gave employment to dozens of servants. Tenant labourers who worked the land were, to a considerable degree, at the mercy of their landlords. Typical farms in west Galway

---

Facing page: Kylemore Lodge.

THE BEGINNING OF KYLEMORE CASTLE.

Connemara in the nineteenth century.

in the mid-nineteenth century were small in size (five to fifteen acres) and each farmer had a cow, a pig and a few sheep.[4] Some families were involved in kelp making, sea fishing and basket making. The area was mainly populated by monoglot Irish speakers, literacy levels were low and there was little formal schooling. In the 1820s, a road-building scheme opened up parts of west Mayo and west Galway, and small piers around the coastline were developed.[5] Relief works operated by the government, and by some local groups, included the construction of a road from Letterfrack to Renvyle. People migrated towards the road-building areas to find work.

Religions, Education and the Development of West Galway

Education in the Archdiocese of Tuam was somewhat ad hoc at the start of the nineteenth century. Landlords on some large estates tried to provide tuition for the children of their labourers and some Protestant landlords recognised that Catholic educators would be more acceptable to many of their tenants. For example, the Third Order of St Francis (Franciscans) were invited to Mountbellew in 1818 by Christopher Grattan Bellew, the local landlord, to educate the poor.[6] In Carna, a Presbyterian, Major Forbes, offered his home to the Mercy Sisters to start a school when he returned to England.[7] Education was also provided by Protestant education societies, such as the Irish Church Missions, whose mission was overtly proselytising.

Nevertheless, attendance at school was low; in 1834, it was calculated that only 12 per cent of the school-age population in the Clifden deanery was enrolled in a school.[8] This was despite the fact that, three years earlier, a state-funded non-denominational system of National Education had been established in Ireland.[9] In the Archdiocese of Tuam, however, this new system was denounced by Archbishop McHale, who perceived it as anti-Catholic.[10] Throughout his long period as archbishop, he refused to co-operate with those who wanted to establish non-denominational schools and prevented their success in west Galway. Instead, he encouraged the expansion of Catholic religious orders, such as the Sisters of Mercy and the Franciscan Brothers. For example, the Sisters of Mercy opened a school for the poor in Castlebar in 1854 and an orphanage in Tuam in 1860. By 1861, they were running a free school, a pay school and an orphanage in Clifden. A few years later, they opened another convent and school in Ballinrobe.[11]

Despite some improvements in education provision, west Galway and west Mayo experienced persistent poverty and unemployment which, together with the devastating impact of several famines, forced thousands of people to emigrate, sometimes with the aid of emigration societies. The second half of the nineteenth century witnessed dramatic population decline in west Connaught: a wave of emigration followed the famine of 1877–9, during which some 10,000 westerners were 'removed under the supervision of the Quaker banker, James Hack Tuke'.[12]

Famine, poor harvests and evictions also resulted in widespread dissatisfaction in Irish rural life. In 1879, the Irish National Land League was founded, under the leadership of Charles Stewart Parnell and Michael Davitt, with the aim of reducing rents and convincing the government that tenant proprietorship was the best way to improve the lot of the rural poor. In Clifden, a branch of the Land League was formed in September 1879, and in 1880 a branch was formed in Letterfrack, close to Kylemore. In 1881, Gladstone's Land Act was passed, granting 'the three Fs': fair rent, fixity of tenure and free sale. The Irish Land Commission was formed and authorised to advance capital to tenants, to help them purchase their holdings. The Land Commission, together with the Congested Districts Board which was established in 1891, brought about a change of land ownership in many parts of the West, though in Connemara the transfer of land proprietorship from landlord to tenant had limited success.

It was against this backdrop of political unease, famine, emigration and social change that Mitchell Henry, the English-born son of Irish parents, purchased the Kylemore estate and began a programme of land reform that would eventually be continued by the Benedictine nuns and that would have a lasting impact on the surrounding area.

Facing page: Mitchell Henry.

MITCHELL HENRY.

Mitchell Henry and Kylemore Castle

Mitchell Henry was a successful Harley Street eye surgeon when, in 1849, he married Margaret Vaughan in Dublin. Margaret was born in County Down; Mitchell was born in Manchester of Irish parents who also came from County Down. Their roots in Ireland were deep; Mitchell Henry's family had lived and worked in Ireland for centuries and he was at pains to point out that he had only Irish blood in him. The couple visited Connemara on their honeymoon and in the decade that followed they made further visits and got to know its people. Meanwhile, Mitchell's reputation as a surgeon was growing. He was a Fellow of the Royal College of Surgeons, Assistant-Surgeon and Lecturer on Morbid Anatomy at the Middlesex Hospital and Surgeon to the North London Infirmary for the Diseases of the Eye.[13] He and

Margaret made their home in London and had four children there in the first decade of their marriage.

In 1862, Mitchell Henry came into a substantial inheritance upon the death of his father, Alexander Henry, who had made a fortune from the cotton trade. Alexander had emigrated from Ireland to Philadelphia in the late eighteenth century, to work with his uncle and to learn about marketing and trading cotton products. He moved to England in 1804, to develop his business, A. and S. Henry & Co. By the time Alexander

From left to right: The gardens developed at Kylemore Castle by Mitchell Henry. Glasshouses on the Kylemore Estate. Palm house on the Kylemore Estate.

Henry died in 1862, his company had expanded to include branches in Bradford, Leeds, Glasgow, Huddersfield, Belfast and Dundee. Mitchell Henry found himself a very wealthy man, who could indulge some of his interests: fine arts, architecture and philanthropy. In 1864, he purchased the freehold of the Stratheden House and Kent House estate, in Knightsbridge, London. There he commenced an elaborate transformation of Stratheden House, purchasing valuable sculptures and paintings for the house and creating an elaborate library with green silk-hung walls, ebonised woodwork and gold mouldings. The house included its own Pompeian-style temple and no expense was spared on the decoration of the rooms, which was overseen by the architect and decorator, Frederick Sang.

When Mitchell and Margaret Henry bought the vast Kylemore estate on 31 December 1866, the house was substantial but more in the character of a fine fishing lodge; the Henrys decided to build a castle around the lodge, embracing it into a dramatic neo-gothic edifice. Mitchell Henry employed a steward, Archibald MacAlister, a Catholic from County Antrim, who was in charge of all the land improvements. He also hired the architect and engineer Samuel Ussher Roberts to design the castle. With a facade built of granite, transported by sea from Dalkey to Letterfrack, the castle was to include 'thirty-three bed and dressing rooms', four bathrooms and several drawing rooms.[14] There was also extensive accommodation for servants. In anticipation of entertaining guests, the Henrys had a ballroom, billiard room, gun room and smoking room included in the design. And to benefit their young family, they also included a school room, library and study.

Immediately surrounding the castle, the Henrys made several developments, including the creation of a fine walled garden which provided fruit, vegetables and flowers for the house. A 'magnificent range of ornamental glasshouses' was constructed, in which was developed a vinery, fernery, banana house, fig house, peach house, conservatory, nectarine house and melon house.[15] Fruits never before grown in this

Mitchell Henry with eight of his children (taken by Alexander George *c*.1877).
Back, from left to right: John Lewis, Mitchell, Forward Howard, Maria.
Front, from left to right: Margaret, Violet, Florence, Geraldine (seated) and
Lorenzo.

Facing page: Geraldine Henry presented at Court (1885).
Above: Kylemore Castle drawing room.

corner of the country were served at the family table, to the delight of guests and neighbouring children, including Ellen Blake of Renvyle House.[16]

The services in the castle included gas lighting, lifts to the upper floors and fire hydrants. A 'fully-equipped Turkish bath' was constructed, containing 'hot and intermediate rooms ... shampooing room ... cooling and dressing room ... [and] fitted lavatory'.[17] Within the precincts of the grounds, there was stabling for twelve horses, a post and telegraph office, fish hatcheries and oyster beds, and 'excellent and varied shooting' was

Kylemore volunteer fire brigade.

available. There was sea access that facilitated 'lobster, trawl and other net fishing' and salmon could be fished 'practically from the door of the castle'.[18] Construction at the castle was completed in 1871 and cost in excess of £29,000.

When they bought the Kylemore estate, there were about 125 sitting tenants, so the Henrys became landlords; this was a role in which they took some pride. As well as employing tenants on his many development schemes, Mitchell Henry also offered them longer leases and helped them to improve their own holdings. He was successful at reclaiming bog land, producing detailed evidence for his methodologies, and he oversaw a system of five-year rotation of crops, to ensure that arable land continued to improve. The Henrys were considered to be good employers and took an interest in their tenants. In 1871, they held a fireworks display and ball at Kylemore Castle, 'to which the tenantry and the numerous tradesmen employed on the estate were invited by Mrs Henry'.[19] By 1877, there were some 240 labourers on the estate.[20]

Henry continued to pursue his political interests and he represented Galway at Westminster from 1871 until 1885. During that time he spoke in the House of Commons at all debates that touched on Ireland, supporting the Irish against what he saw as the injustices of the British crown: 'Augment your Army you may, stretch your coercion laws you can; but there is one thing you cannot do – refuse justice and maintain your Empire in peace.'[21]

At Westminster, Henry also spoke out against absentee English landlords, whose treatment of their tenants in Connemara kept them in abject poverty, and he berated the House for taking no action against these landlords:

> There were thousands of poor people in Ireland who did not taste butcher's meat more than two or three times in a year, but who lived in a chronic state of starvation. A landlord had no right to raise rents ... Mr Buckley, by his conduct as a landowner, had reduced his tenantry to the condition of the fellaheen of Egypt – the most miserable peasantry in the world – who toiled for earnings which were instantly swallowed up in the payment of taxes ... these cases had no parallel in England, where the poorest labourer was better off than his fellow in Ireland.[22]

In addition to making many improvements on the Kylemore estate, Henry took an interest in the education of his tenants' children. As a father of a growing brood (the Henrys eventually had nine children) he demonstated the education interests of a man of his rank: he kept tutors for the young children, brought them on educational trips, including a tour to Egypt, and sent his sons to Eton, Cambridge and Oxford. To extend the benefits of education to his tenants, he built a school in Lettergesh in 1868. For poor Catholics, the school offered an alternative to the proselytising schools run by the Irish Church Mission, where food and clothing were given to pupils in an attempt to encourage them to convert to Protestantism. Mitchell Henry opposed proselytism in all its forms and spoke at Westminster of the rights of Catholics to a Catholic education, saying: 'Roman Catholics constitute four-fifths of the Irish nation … They have an indefeasible right to educate their children as they think right – not as other people think right.'[23]

The school at Lettergesh followed one of the architectural designs approved by the Commissioners for National Education in Ireland. It was made of stone, with a slate roof, and had separate classrooms for boys and girls. The additional buildings greatly enhanced the school and made it an attractive place to teach. These comprised 'a four-roomed schoolmaster's house, also of stone and slate, and a two-roomed stone and corrugated iron roofed schoolmistress's bungalow'.[24] Two Catholic school teachers were hired.

Henry was attracted to the principles behind the National System, formed in 1831, which supported non-denominational schooling. Existing schools could become affiliated to the National Board, and benefit from grants and materials, if they were conducted under the regulations of the Board. Pupils of all faiths were given secular instruction together, but religious instruction had to be provided separately, through visits from priests and ministers. In principle, the system afforded a free non-denominational education to all children. But in practice, because passages from scripture were used in national school textbooks and the Bible was read in some schools, some of the Roman Catholic hierarchy expressed serious concerns that national schools were not non-denominational. The Archbishop of Tuam, Dr McHale, refused to allow Catholic teachers to train at the non-denominational teacher training college at Marlborough Street, in Dublin, and he would not allow the convent national schools in his archdiocese to benefit from state aid. Additionally, he gave directives to close all of the national schools in Aughavale parish that were established with the support of the local landlord, the Marquess of Sligo.[25] Unsurprisingly, when the local Roman Catholic priest was offered the position of school manager by Mitchell Henry, he had to turn it down.

After several years of hard work on his vast estate, Mitchell Henry planned an exotic trip for his family. November 1874 saw the Henrys embark on a tour of Egypt, bringing with them some of their children. The party was large and included friends, as well as several servants, a nurse, a nanny and a tutor for the children. Travel to Egypt had become fashionable for the leisured and wealthy classes following the opening of the Suez Canal in 1870. The Prince and Princess of Wales had made a visit there in 1869 and the British aristocracy and gentry were becoming gripped by 'Egyptomania'. Armed with copies of Murray's *Guidebook to Modern Egypt and Thebes*, they employed couriers, who arranged all the details of the trip. Fashionable tourists used exclusive accommodation, such as Shepheard's Hotel in Cairo, from which they could watch the daily ebb and flow of crowds, 'a noisy, changing, restless, part-coloured tide, half European, half Oriental, on foot, on horseback and in carriages'.[26] And a wealthy tourist could hire his own dragoman (a kind of agent) and charter a private barge-like boat, or *dahabeeah*, to sail the Nile. By the time the Henrys were touring in Egypt, the most luxurious of these vessels were furnished with china, crystal, Brussels carpets, fine furniture and mirrors. But cooking was done on deck and there was little awareness of how contaminated food or dirty water could cause illnesses. Western tourists, including those who went to Egypt for a 'cure' for tuberculosis, sometimes contracted fatal diseases.

While Mitchell Henry made every possible plan for a comfortable and educational trip to Egypt, the expedition was to be a turning point in his life, heralding a period of deep sadness. At the end of November, his beloved wife, Margaret, contracted dysentry. The infection, which would have resulted in chronic diarrhoea, was usually spread by polluted water and by flies. Common treatments at that time were the use of opium, warm baths and 'blood letting', but doctors generally admitted that they had a poor understanding of the infection. The seriousness of the illness would have been known to the Henrys and indeed, it had been widespread in the famine-afflicted areas of Ireland in the mid-nineteenth century. Margaret Henry died on 4 December. Her death had a profound and lasting effect on her husband. He had her body embalmed, refusing to agree to a burial until the following spring when the remains were brought back to Connemara.[27]

In the 1870s, bad weather and crop failure would bring west Galway to near famine again. Land agitation had begun in earnest, involving demand for rent reduction and relief. In 1879, the Clifden branch of the Land League was founded and a year later a branch was founded in Letterfrack. Rents were boycotted on the Henry estate and on other nearby estates, including that of the Blakes, at Renvyle.[28] Although Mitchell Henry withdrew his support of the Land League, he made some concessions in favour of his tenants. In September 1879, he gave them a remission of half a year's rent, concluding: 'I trust that this arrangement will tide us over our difficulties.'[29] He also spoke out in favour of security of tenure and urged other landlords to reduce rents to a fair level, but he was not a supporter of the increasing demands for peasant proprietorship. However, rent concessions were insufficient in

---

Facing page: Kylemore Estate staff.

west Galway, in the face of poor harvests, starvation and the prospect of the bailiff. By 1882, hundreds had been evicted in Connemara for non-payment of rent. In the months of April and May alone, 1,300 people – mostly from Clifden – emigrated under the emigration schemes put in place by the Quaker James Hack Tuke. By 1884, Tuke's emigration schemes had assisted 9,482 people to leave for North America, greatly depleting the population of Clifden.

Meanwhile, although rent reductions on the Kylemore estate must have had some impact on Mitchell Henry's bank account, his lifestyle continued seemingly unaffected. The staff at his London home included a German governess; an English housekeeper; three ladies' maids, two French and one English; a German seamstress; three kitchen maids; four housemaids; an English butler; a French cook; an odd-job man; an under butler; two footmen; and a carpenter.[30] At Kylemore, the Henrys kept an indoor and outdoor staff, including gillies, grooms and farm labourers, while the younger children had a nanny, maids and a governess. There were also costs attached to the schooling of his sons at Eton, after which one went up to Oxford in 1869 and another to Cambridge in 1878.

Eventually, the upkeep of his homes drained Mitchell Henry's fortune and his income may also have been depleted by losses on investments in mining, in both South Africa and Australia.[31] In 1902, estate agents in London and Dublin announced that 'Kylemore Abbey in the heart of Connemara' was for sale, noting its proximity to 'the Atlantic Coast'.[32] The domain included twelve townlands, extensive fishing rights and a harbour in which yachts, up to 200 tons, could be moored.[33] At the sale

---

Facing page, from top:
Kylemore Castle, a large catch.
Kylemore Castle gun room.

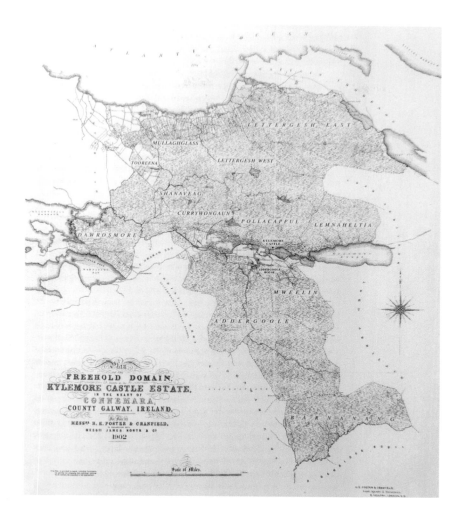

Facing page: Auction catalogue for the sale of Kylemore Castle (1902).

Above: Map of the freehold domain known as the Kylemore Castle Estate (1902).

Facing page: Duke and Duchess of Manchester, Kylemore Castle.
Above: Duchess of Manchester with some of the Henry family.

of the entire domain, comprising 13,000 acres, the estate was described as 'one of the grandest Domains in the British Isles and one worthy of Royal occupation'.[34] By 1903, the estate had been taken over by William Angus Drogo Montague, 9th Duke of Manchester, who had married an American heiress, Helena Zimmerman, in 1900.

The Duke of Manchester's self-confessed gambling addiction, together with his lavish tastes, put Kylemore in jeopardy from the start. Declared bankrupt at the age of twenty-three, the Duke had been bailed out by his millionaire father-in-law within days of his marriage to Helena. Neither did the Duke's racism augur well for the tenants and staff on the Kylemore estate. His crude classification of 'the Irish race' included a category that he called 'the mongrel', which he described as being 'sly, cruel, deceitful, lazy'.[35] He compensated for his lack of interest in the estate by spending large amounts on the house, especially when, in 1904, a return visit of King Edward was proposed.[36]

In preparation for the royal visit, the Duchess undertook extensive renovations to Kylemore Castle, spending some of her father's fortune as she removed some of the castle's finest features. One of the most striking changes was the removal of the marble arches in the hallway and the insertion of mock Jacobean wood panelling on the walls. Mitchell Henry's library and study were transformed into one large reception hall, stained glass windows were removed and the Gothic ballroom was replaced with a large kitchen.[37] In the event, the King did not pay this return visit to Kylemore.

As a consequence of extravagance and financial difficulties, the Duke and Duchess lost their Kylemore home. The Duchess's father, Eugene Zimmerman, took over the mortgage on the entire estate in 1910, but when he died, in 1914, the mortgage was still outstanding. While Zimmerman left a fortune to his daughter, she did not choose to keep the estate.

The mortgage was taken over by a London banker and property speculator, Ernest John Fawke, who did not take up residence in the castle.[38] Fawke doubtless hoped to make a profit on the break-up and sale of the estate but he was unsucessful in this. The outbreak of the First World War and the changing political landscape at home in Ireland left the London banker with little prospect of finding a buyer and tenants looked on helplessly as the estate went into decline.

In December 1920, the castle and estate at Kylemore were finally sold. News soon spread in the locality that the new owners were the Irish

Benedictine Dames of Ypres. It is not idle speculation to suggest that, at that point in the history of the nation and of the Catholic Church in Ireland, the new owners were a welcome addition to the Archdiocese of Tuam and the deanery of Clifden.

A new era in the history of the Kylemore estate was about to begin.

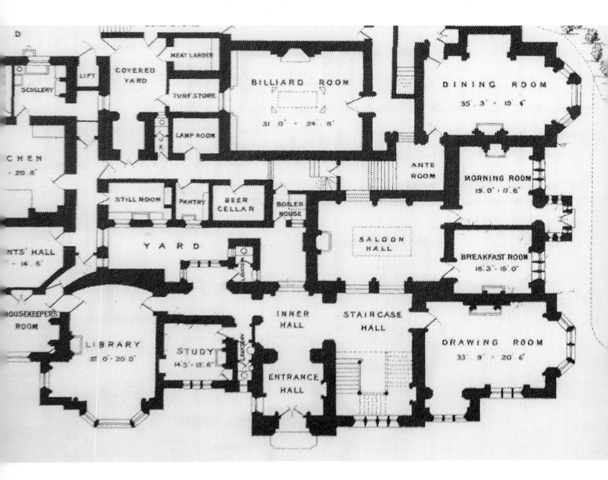

Above and overleaf: Ground plan of Kylemore Castle (1902).

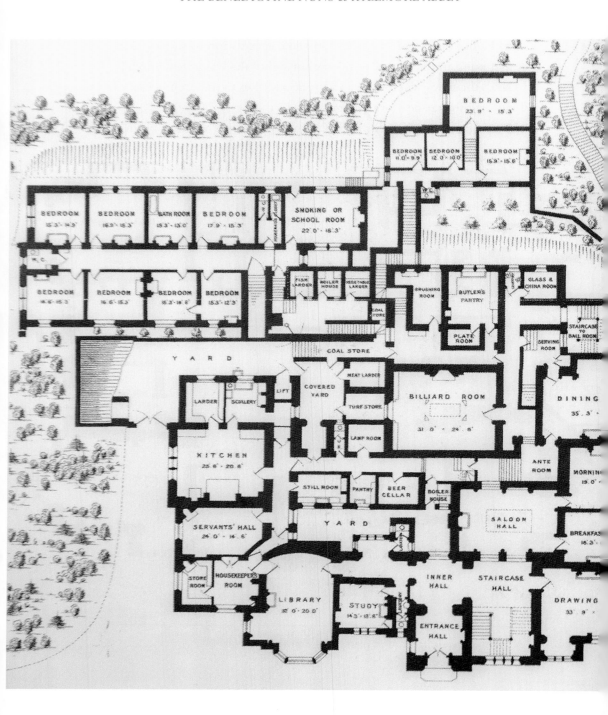

BEDROOM
23'.8" - 15'.3"

BEDROOM
11'.0" - 9'.9"

BEDROOM
12'.0" - 10'.0"

BEDROOM
15'.3" - 15'.6"

BEDROOM
15'.3" - 14'.9"

BEDROOM
16'.3" - 15'.3"

BATH ROOM
15'.3" - 13'.0"

BEDROOM
17'.9" - 15'.3"

SMOKING OR
SCHOOL ROOM
22'.0" - 15'.3"

W.C.

BEDROOM
14'.6" - 15'.3"

BEDROOM
16'.6" - 15'.3"

BEDROOM
15'.3" - 14'.6"

BEDROOM
15'.3" - 12'.3"

FISH
LARDER

BOILER
HOUSE

VEGETABLE
LARDER

BRUSHING
ROOM

BUTLER'S
PANTRY

GLASS &
CHINA ROOM

COAL
STORE

PLATE
ROOM

STAIRCASE
TO BALL ROOM

SERVING
ROOM

YARD

COAL STORE

MEAT LARDER

BILLIARD ROOM
31'.0" - 24'.6"

DINING
35'.3"

LARDER

SCULLERY

LIFT

COVERED
YARD

TURF STORE

LAMP ROOM

KITCHEN
25'.6" - 20'.6"

ANTE
ROOM

MORNING
15'.0"

STILL ROOM

PANTRY

BEER
CELLAR

BOILER
HOUSE

SALOON
HALL

SERVANTS' HALL
24'.0" - 14'.6"

YARD

BREAKFAST
16'.3"

STORE
ROOM

HOUSEKEEPERS
ROOM

LIBRARY
27'.0" - 20'.0"

STUDY
14'.3" - 13'.6"

INNER
HALL

STAIRCASE
HALL

DRAWING
33'.9"

ENTRANCE
HALL

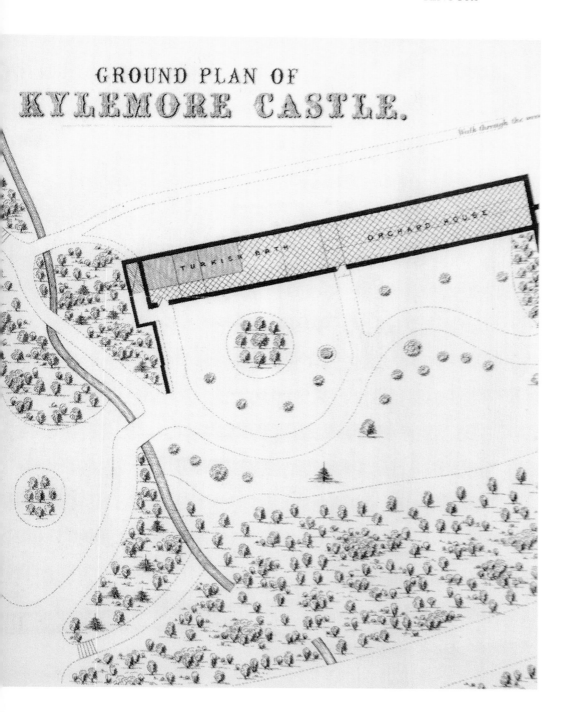

Visit of King Edward VII to Kylemore Castle, 1903.

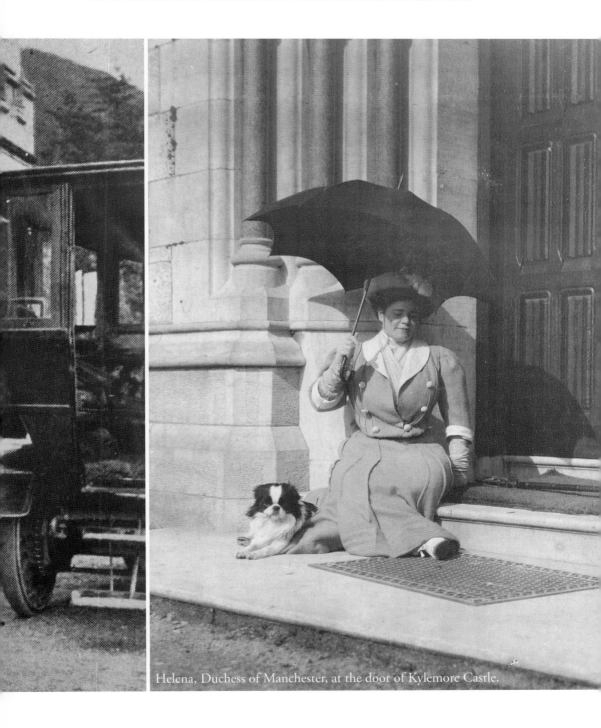

Helena, Duchess of Manchester, at the door of Kylemore Castle.

Pupils at Kylemore Abbey (undated)

LABORA

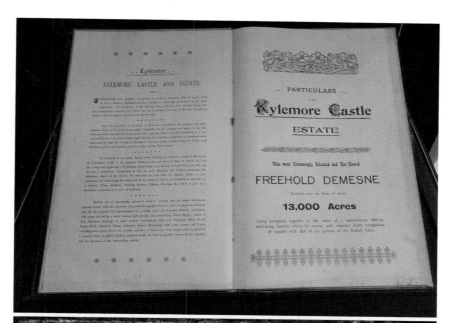

Sr Magdalena FitzGibbon

Mother Máire Hickey

Sr Marie Genevieve Mukamana, Sr Genevieve Harrington and Sr Aidan Ryan packaging Kylemore Abbey soap.

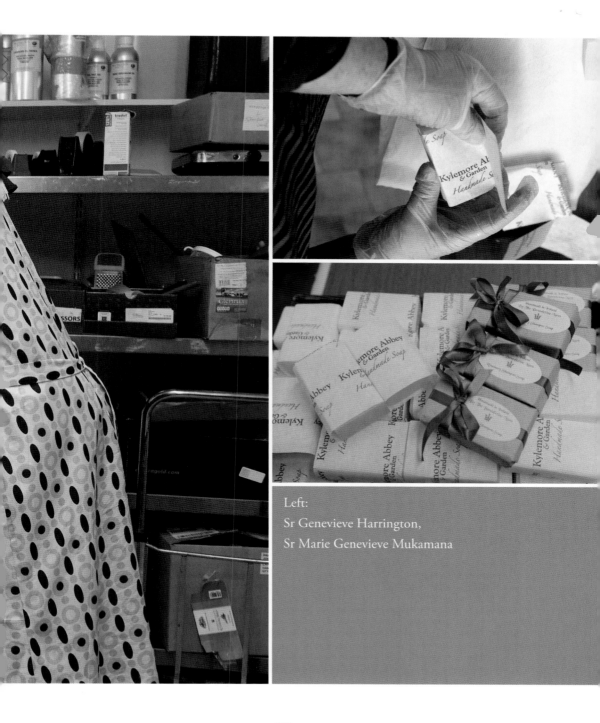

Left:
Sr Genevieve Harrington,
Sr Marie Genevieve Mukamana

Sr Genevieve Harrington

Facing page: Sr Dorothy Ryan
Above: Sr Noreen Gallagher

Sr Karol O'Connell and Darragh Michel (pupil)

Sr Karol O'Connell

*'Therefore we intend to establish
a school for the Lord's service.'*

St Benedict (AD 480–547)

CHAPTER FOUR
THE BENEDICTINES AT KYLEMORE ABBEY, 1920–1959

The purchase of Kylemore Castle as the new abbey for the Irish Dames of Ypres involved a large financial commitment on the part of the Benedictines. Although they had managed to acquire the property for about one-third of the original asking price of £150,000, nevertheless, they needed a great deal of help. While they had the support of generous benefactors and guarantors of the loan, their next great task was to find means of sustenance for the community and the wherewith to pay the yearly interest on the loan – a not inconsiderable sum. The farm had to be stocked, the school had to be equipped and staff had to be paid.

Throughout the following decades, the nuns were creative in finding ways of sustaining themselves and also in preserving and enhancing the property they had acquired. The establishment of a school was the first priority, as a continuation of the history of their monastery in Belgium, which had provided education for girls for centuries. Indeed, the roll for their school in County Wexford was headed: 'Pupils Educated at the Ypres Benedictine Abbey, Merton 1916'.[1] The same roll book continued to be used when the school at Kylemore eventually opened, indicating

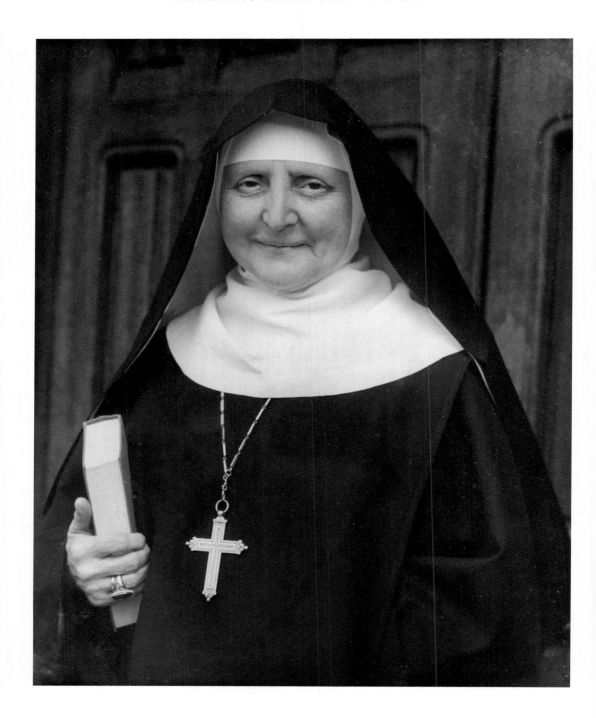

the wish of the nuns that there should be an almost seamless connection between the schools in Ypres, Wexford and Connemara.

The key person in the establishment of the school was Dame Scholastica Murphy and she became the first headmistress. Educated by the Dominicans in Eccles Street, she had gone on to qualify as a teacher in London.[2] Ellen Murphy entered the Benedictine monastery at Macmine, where she was professed in 1920. She was recognised by all as highly intelligent and past pupils recalled her ability and her magnanimity. A brilliant teacher and a gifted administrator, her talents combined to make her a very successful headmistress. Her pupils, who credited her with the ability to see through walls and around corners, held her in affectionate regard. Many remained in contact with her when they had finished school and their letters give some insight into the atmosphere that Dame Scholastica created at Kylemore in its early years. One wrote to her to say: 'I often wish I were back at school again in Kylemore ... I think that my last year at school was one of the happiest I ever spent.'[3] Another pupil echoed the sentiment in a letter to Dame Scholastica, concluding: 'I often think of past happy and jolly days with my old school-fellows and sometimes almost wish them over again.'[4]

The school opened on 16 January 1921.[5] Throughout the first two years, the school began to attract pupils, some of whom had a connection with the nuns. For example, the nuns noted in the roll book that Patricia Kelly from Dublin, who enrolled in April 1921, was the 'eldest daughter of Cissie Barton, one of our Ypres pupils'.[6] Unsurprisingly, siblings were often enrolled together. Shirley and Muriel Robinson arrived from England, the three Flinn sisters came from Dublin (aged between 8 and 10) and there were several pairs of sisters from Waterford and Limerick, in addition to girls who came from Navan, Tuam and Kells.[7]

Facing page: Lady Abbess Maura Ostyn (1916–40), 1920s.

To secure pupils and promote the school, Dame Scholastica was enterprising in her efforts. She put a 'splash advert' in a Kerry newspaper and had an annual calendar made, with an image of Kylemore, which she sent far and wide.[8] By 1925, a Dublin parent wrote to tell her: 'You are wonderful and your name has become famous in connection with Kylemore.'[9] Dame Scholastica was particularly adept at networking with people in Galway city, writing to members of the university and to prominent business people to invite them to the annual Christmas concert. Even when they could not make the long journey out to Kylemore, people were supportive of the school. For example, when bad weather prevented the O'Gorman printing family from attending the Christmas concert in 1925, they sent on 'a prize for the youngest girl in the entertainment'.[10] When the Department of Education made its first inspection of Kylemore Abbey school (1924–5), it found that the school was 'well organized … [with] good accommodation for the pupils … [and] the curriculum is balanced and comprehensive'.[11]

Though Dame Scholastica worked relentlessly to recruit pupils, there were some obstacles that proved hard to overcome. Firstly, Kylemore had to compete with many other convent schools, including those with lower fees. Even attracting girls from the county was a challenge, as there were five other recognised convent secondary schools in County Galway by the mid-1920s.[12] When an appeal was made to Br Hogan, at the novitiate of the Irish Christian Brothers, to help spread word of Kylemore amongst Dublin parents, he answered plainly:

> I have not lost sight of my promise of doing what I can to procure girls for the school, but … I am not at all in touch with the class of parents who would, and who could, afford the pension required by the pupils attending your school, and who at the same time would expect a more practical course of education for their girls, and whose future will probably depend on their education …[13]

Another difficulty was the significant travel involved in getting to Kylemore, at a time when 'young ladies' did not travel about the country without a chaperone. A letter to Dame Scholastica, criticising the travel arrangements for pupils, noted that:

> There were no reserved compartments to Broadstone, so the children were 'on their own' practically from Galway … in the carriages they were scattered among people of the world. We could not get accommodation for them all together.[14]

Despite the challenges attached to recruiting girls to a Connemara convent, the school was, by all standards, a successful school. From the very beginning, music was an important subject on the curriculum and an examiner from the Royal Irish Academy of Music came annually to examine the girls. He managed the complicated logistics of travel by giving clear instructions to Dame Scholastica:

> Signor Esposito and I are to examine in Galway on Monday April 6th. I leave Galway on Tuesday 7th April in the middle of the day, could you send to meet me at Recess … I could then examine all your candidates and also your Intermediate Choir. Afterwards I would need to go on to Clifden to examine, so should ask you to motor me to Recess on Tuesday eve., or to Clifden, which ever would be most convenient.[15]

Extending Benedictine hospitality, Dame Scholastica invited Mr Weaving to stay overnight and he graciously accepted her hospitality.[16]

Academic success was also a hallmark of the school. From the beginning, careers and studies pursued by past pupils suggest that they had received a good academic grounding. By 1926, a Kylemore past-pupil was undertaking a medical degree in Dublin, while another 'passed Trinity Matric in September and … intends doing Law after Christmas'.[17]

For local girls, a domestic economy school, known as St Maur's, was set up in the early 1930s. It was later replaced by a secondary day school called Scoil Áine.

Funding and Expansion

Despite the success of the school, both in terms of the personal happiness of the pupils and their academic achievement, the numbers remained low, partly because of the slump caused by the difficulties of transport during the Second World War, from which the school was slow to recover. As late as June 1955, three partial scholarships were offered so as to help in the building up of the numbers in the school. For these, examination centres were held in Dublin and Kylemore.[18] Nevertheless, 'the boarding school opened on 9th September [1955] with seventeen pupils'.[19] That year, Dame Mary O'Toole, who had been appointed as headmistress, was 'replaced by Mother Prioress while Dame Mary attended the University in Galway'.[20]

But the Abbey had been struggling from the start and the nuns were constantly trying to find ways of making money. A meeting of Council in August 1929 recorded:

> Lady Abbess made known that two ladies had applied for Board and lodging. She had consulted Rev Fr Harrington who considered that in our present circumstances the opportunity was a golden one to help financially. Therefore she had decided to accept them. The Bungalow is to be put at their disposal and they have agreed to take on themselves the expense of adding another small room. All agreed to this arrangement.[21]

However, the small income that could be generated from taking on new tenants was not enough to defray mounting expenses. There were also other challenges for the community, who – on an estate as vast as

Dame Teresa Howard (back left), Abbess Maura Ostyn (back centre), Dame Elizabeth Magdalen Lee (back right) with Rajkumary Rajendra Kumari (front left) and Rajkumary Manher Kumari (front right) of Jamnager, boarders in the 1930s.

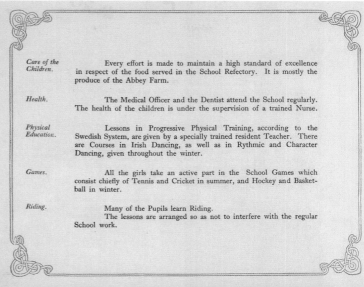

Care of the Children.	Every effort is made to maintain a high standard of excellence in respect of the food served in the School Refectory. It is mostly the produce of the Abbey Farm.
Health.	The Medical Officer and the Dentist attend the School regularly. The health of the children is under the supervision of a trained Nurse.
Physical Education.	Lessons in Progressive Physical Training, according to the Swedish System, are given by a specially trained resident Teacher. There are Courses in Irish Dancing, as well as in Rythmic and Character Dancing, given throughout the winter.
Games.	All the girls take an active part in the School Games which consist chiefly of Tennis and Cricket in summer, and Hockey and Basket-ball in winter.
Riding.	Many of the Pupils learn Riding. The lessons are arranged so as not to interfere with the regular School work.

Clockwise from left:

Kylemore Abbey Refectory.

Kylemore Abbey Prospectus (early 20th century).

Kylemore Abbey School Choir, June 1925.

141

Pupils at the front door of Kylemore Abbey, early 1930s.

Kylemore – could not erect a boundary wall and create a traditional form of enclosure. The Archbishop of Tuam, Dr Thomas Gilmartin, had suggested to the nuns that they should consider the mountains around them to be their enclosure.[22] It was not a fanciful suggestion; the remoteness of Kylemore Abbey and the mountainous landscape that grew up around the estate – and especially the wall of mountain behind the Abbey itself – certainly served to create a sense of separation from the wider world. But the activities of the farm, the comings and goings of workers, the curious visitors who ventured up the avenue to see the beautiful Abbey and the distance between the Abbey and the Gothic Church suggested that it was not an ideal place for a monastic community. An Apostolic Visitation had resulted in a suggestion that the Abbey should be sold and a more suitable place should be found. By November 1929, a meeting of the Chapter discussed the issue of selling Kylemore and the Lady Abbess advised:

> You remember that the Apostolic Visitors considered Kylemore very unsuitable for Benedictine nuns. The distance between the convent and the farm. The impossibility of control. The question of Enclosure and regular discipline, has led to the conclusion that I have to announce to you that the Holy See has directed me to sell Kylemore and to seek for a more suitable and central place … It goes without saying that there will be no difficulty in getting a suitable place, but our difficulty is in selling Kylemore; everything depends on the sale.[23]

Various legal and other arguments ensued, and the final outcome was that Kylemore continued as a Benedictine Abbey. Another threat to the Abbey came in the 1950s, when it was proposed to found a Dublin house because, according to those making the proposal, 'Kylemore had come to naught financially'.[24] Some of the community wanted to join such a Dublin house. However, the Council did not approve the proposal. Council minutes record a decision that anyone leaving Kylemore to be part of this proposed Dublin abbey would forfeit 'all capitular and other rights as regards Kylemore' and could not take anything with them from Kylemore 'except their own personal clothes and choir books'.[25]

Throughout the 1950s, the nuns attempted, by various innovations, to address their poor financial situation. They leased cottages on the estate; they purchased a lorry, which was 'a great saving in drawing wood

Above: The nuns collecting their own turf, 1936.

Right: Feeding the chickens at Addergoole Farm, 1930s.

Left: St Maur's Domestic School, 1930s.

and turf to the Abbey'.[26] They were given a gift of a manual knitting machine and training in its use, so that they could make garments under the label 'Made in Kylemore'.[27] They also looked at practical solutions for supporting such a vast estate, including cutting and selling timber and, in the summer months, they ran a guest house. The guest house, which could have accommodated up to sixty people, became a noted success not least because of the attraction of the fishing rights on the estate.

In 1952, the nuns agreed to raise the dowry from £300 to £500; they also raised the fees for the maintenance of postulants and novices.[28] However, the requirement for a dowry was never used as a reason for

refusing entry to a candidate for religious life. Where a postulant could not afford the dowry, concessions were made. For example, in 1954, an entrant had her dowry rate reduced 'by one-third of the prescribed dowry'.[29] Also, dowries were returned if women left.[30] And the Benedictine hospitality continued, despite their financial difficulties. For example, in December 1952, Dame Veronica came from Oulton to stay at Kylemore 'as a guest, so as not to be held down by the observance. This would give her freedom for rest ...'. The Kylemore nuns were 'glad to be able to do this favour for the Oulton nuns who were so good to [them] when [they] went to the Oulton Community after leaving Ypres in 1914'.[31]

When Dame Bernard Stewart took up the role of headmistress, she began the negotiation to have a day school, Scoil Áine, recognised by the Department of Education. The day school not only offset the fall in pupil numbers in the boarding school during the Second World War but it also made a contribution to girls' education in the locality at that time. Teresa Lydon, who attended Kylemore Abbey from 1939 until 1944, recalled:

> We walked to school ... during the war years, it was physically impossible to get tyres for the bikes ... Even to cycle in to Galway that time, to go to school in Dominican College or the Convent of Mercy ... there was no transport, it was physically impossible ... We had the Gregorian chants and we had the choir and it was really lovely ... it [was] such a lovely privilege to go up for a quiet prayer into the chapel, and hear the nuns, it was beautiful ... how happy we were, there was that absolute exuberance, it was gorgeous.[32]

Facing page: Saving the hay at Kylemore Abbey.

Facing page: Lady Abbess Placid Druhan (1941–53).

Above: Lady Abbess Placid Druhan with Archbishop Joseph Walsh, the Kylemore community and five first holy communicants, 1941.

Other families who lived on the estate also attended the school, including Nora and Eileen Joyce, who walked to school from Currywongane, and the girls recalled the plentiful food, Benedictine hospitality and the daily example of the nuns:

> Mostly we went over the shortcut where the new gardens are now … If we were in study late, they arranged for us to be accompanied … You'd get good luscious food, vegetables … fish … lamb … You had this beautiful location, this beautiful communion with nature, you had this community of nuns … [and] a continental influence. Loads of deportment and decorum …[33]

Maeve O'Beirne (later Sr Benedict), who was sent to the junior school 'as a very junior junior' in 1938 to avoid the threat of war brewing in Europe, considered the school to have been 'much more unconventional than other schools'.[34] Indeed, it was for this reason that her father, a lecturer in criminal law at Cambridge, chose Kylemore for his daughter. He 'liked the relative freedom of the school'.[35] Sr Benedict recalled her schooldays, saying that Kylemore

> was non-regimented and there was nothing rigid about it. You weren't made to play games. When there were enough to make a team the gamey ones played tennis or other sports and the rest of us just pushed out into the woods. Dame Bernard and a couple of other nuns took us on interesting walks.[36]

She also recalled that 'Dame Bernard would read parts of the newspapers to the girls, with any relevant War news.'[37]

Other nuns were equally generous in giving time to the pupils. Sr Benedict remembered Dame Magdalen Lee, who 'had been Headmistress of Scoil Áine for a while, and had the most gentle way of correcting one, which was far more effective than a scolding'.[38] Dame Magdalen spent a lot of time with the juniors, supervising meals, study time and recreation. 'She also taught us to recite poetry, mostly choral recitation. Many of the poems she selected were rather above our heads – she was a great admirer of Francis Thompson and Sir Walter Scott.'[39] Dame Bernard equally developed the pupils' love of literature, reading Shakespeare's plays and making a point of reading wider than the prescribed English curriculum. For a bright pupil such as Maeve O'Beirne, the liberal atmosphere of Kylemore was perfect. In due course, Maeve read law at the University of Cambridge and, in 1957, she returned to Kylemore to enter the monastery. On 15 October 1962, she became Dame Benedict.[40]

Tennis at Kylemore Abbey School, 1940s.

Leadership and Religious Life at the Abbey

If Maeve O'Beirne had found her schooling at Kylemore to be 'non-regimented', the same could not be said of the start to her religious life. She recalled: 'The Canonical Year was where you were absolutely incarcerated. If they had a dungeon they would have put you in it.'[41] However, once professed as Dame Benedict, she was allowed to introduce several far-seeing initiatives. She designed a five-year plan for the walled Victorian garden, to develop six acres; she taught horse-riding and she gave tuition to pupils who needed additional support. She also turned her hand to cookery. As the only community member who could drive, it was Dame Benedict who could undertake errands and drive the girls to any necessary appointments. Dame Benedict, whose family owned a

Clockwise from left:

Kylemore Abbey pupils on the strand, *c.*1930s.

Sr Magdalena FitzGibbon mowing the lawn in front of the new noviceship, late 1960s.

Lady Abbess Maura Ostyn with Archbishop T. P. Gilmartin, 1930s.

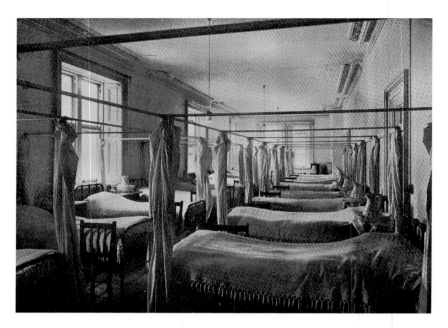

Dormitory at Kylemore Abbey School.

farm, brought considerable farming knowledge to Kylemore. She made the decision to get rid of the flock of sheep that the nuns had been grazing on the Diamond mountain. The sheep were regularly being stolen, so Dame Benedict decided to end that venture. Instead, she got Friesian cows, which supplied the community with milk and butter, and a herd of Charolais cattle for beef. The changes that followed the Second Vatican Council included that nuns could be given permission to attend meetings outside the enclosure. Dame Benedict was allowed to attend fisheries meetings[42] and was elected first president of the Northwest Connemara branch of the Irish Farmers' Association.[43]

Before the Second Vatican Council, Abbesses, once elected, remained in office until their death. Lady Abbess Maura Ostyn, who had guided the monastery on its journey from Macmine and established it in Kylemore in 1920, died in 1940. Dame Placid Druhan was elected to succeed her and received the abbatial blessing on 17 April 1941. 'The occasion was one of great rejoicing for Kylemore, especially as it was exactly 100 years since an Irish Abbess had been given to our community. Lady Abbess Placid was a native of Lady's Island Wexford.'[44] She was twelve years Abbess and was remembered by the nuns as one of 'the great figures in our history, humble, kind and holy'.[45]

Elected in 1953, her successor, Lady Abbess Agnes Finnegan, was the first Abbess who had entered in Ireland. Under her stewardship, the Benedictines continued to attract vocations, including girls they had taught. Though the boarding school was still small, prospects were good and parents spoke highly of their daughters' education.

The modest number of pupils in the boarding school reflected the general state of secondary education at a time when there were only 526 recognised secondary schools in existence, almost all of which were small institutions under private, voluntary management by religious orders.[46] These schools charged fees, which, though sometimes small, were impossible for many families at a time when the birth rate was growing and parents struggled to educate large families.[47] The majority of secondary schools were located in Leinster and Munster, where religious orders were assured of support.[48] Indeed, the annual reports of the Department of Education during the mid-twentieth century indicate the absence of secondary education provision in many rural areas. Connaught had only eighty-four recognised secondary schools, while there were 242 in Leinster and 200 in Munster.[49]

Even when parents wanted to send their daughters to convent day schools, there was almost no public transportation. Boarding schools supplied the demands of middle and upper-middle-class parents, who wanted an academic education for their daughters. They had a number of well-known boarding schools from which they could choose. For example, the Ursulines were well established in Cork and Thurles, the Dominicans took boarders in their Dublin convents and the schools of the Loreto Sisters were flourishing in Dublin, Navan and

Facing page: Sr Benedict O'Beirne.

This page: Milking parlour at the farm.

Overleaf: The devastation caused by the fire, 1959.

Cork. Indeed, some Catholic parents chose to send their daughters to academic Protestant boarding schools, such as Alexandra College. A boarding school like Kylemore, far away from the prosperous Catholic populations of Dublin and Cork, had to struggle to attract boarders to its remote location. Nonetheless, at the close of the 1950s, the nuns at Kylemore Abbey could be satisfied that their tireless work was showing dividends; the reputation of the school was growing and the success of the guest house had given the nuns some financial security. A period of stability was now to be expected.

But just after the abbey entered the final year of its fourth decade in Connemara, disaster struck when a fire broke out.

SUCCISA VIRESCIT

Above: Mother Máire Hickey

Above, from left to right:

Sr Noreen Gallagher, Sr Aidan Ryan, Sr Marie Genevieve Mukamana,
Sr Karol O'Connell, Sr Genevieve Harrington, Mother Máire Hickey,
Sr Dorothy Ryan, Sr Magdalena FitzGibbon, Sr Mary Jiao

'It is not perfection that leads to God, but perseverance.'

Joan Chittister OSB (1936–)

CHAPTER FIVE

GROWTH AND CHANGE AT KYLEMORE ABBEY, 1959–2019

For the Kylemore community, things changed very quickly on 25 January 1959, when fire broke out in the west wing of the Abbey. The community had gone to bed the night before, little suspecting that by daybreak some of their school and monastery would be destroyed. The fire, which started in the sewing room, spread upwards to the kitchen, laundry and dormitory. As the alarm was raised throughout the building, children were brought to safety and some nuns clambered out through French windows. Fire brigades from Clifden, Westport, Castlebar, Loughrea, Gort, Galway, Athenry and Claremorris came to the site as quickly as possible and many locals came out to help fight the fire and save what they could.[1] There was no loss of life and most of the most treasured artefacts were saved, including a piece of lace made by Mary, Queen of Scots, and a portrait of James II. But the damage to the Abbey was extensive and furniture, clothes and a treasured carpet made by Dame Xavier at Ypres were lost.[2]

Dame Mechtilde Moloney, present on the night, later recalled the devastation that they faced as morning broke:

The tower bell melted into thin air … Leaded roofs were no more; stairways, dormitories, guest rooms were in shambles, iron bedsteads hung off the remaining turrets, a sorry sight, but thank God only goods and chattels were caught in the flames.[3]

In the weeks that followed the fire, the nuns had to determine the extent of the damage, working with architects and builders. In the event, it emerged that it was considerable and pupils had to be sent home. There followed a period of careful discernment, to decide whether or not to remain in Kylemore or find a new monastery. At Chapter meetings in February and May, the Lady Abbess asked all those assembled to vote and on both occasions the majority favoured remaining.[4] Initially, they hoped to build a new monastery and reconstruct the castle as a school. The builders, John Sisk and Sons, offered to wait a few years for completion of payment, as the costs were high. However, the nuns could not meet the costs and decided to complete the necessary reconstruction of the castle and move the noviceship and cells to a new extension, thereby allowing space to be freed up for the school. They also decided to close the junior school and guest house, and stop serving lunches and teas to tourists. Instead, they would concentrate their efforts on the boarding school and on running a summer language school, to supplement their income. These decisions reflected the adaptability of the nuns at a challenging and uncertain time. It took three years for the Abbey to be fully restored.

Facing page: Lady Abbess Agnes Finnegan (1953–81).
Overleaf: Kylemore Abbey following the completion of the restoration, c.1963.

Education and Change in the 1960s

Even as the nuns were returning to some kind of normal routine at the Abbey in the early 1960s, changes were in the air for Irish secondary education. Despite the obvious financial and geographical difficulties associated with gaining a second-level education, student enrolments in post-primary schools were growing. In 1940, 38,713 pupils attained second-level education.[5] By 1958, this figure had risen to 69,568 and by 1965 secondary school attendance was 92,989 pupils.[6] The Irish government had produced a *White Paper on Economic Expansion* in 1958, indicating the importance of investment in education and concluding that the 'prosperity of a modern technological society depended on the availability of an educated workforce'.[7] There were further developments in Irish education following an OECD conference in Washington DC, in October 1961, at which two Irish delegates were approached and encouraged to undertake a pilot study of education in Ireland.[8] The Minister for Education, Patrick Hillery, agreed to the study and on 29 July 1962 he appointed a team to carry out the OECD-sponsored survey on Irish secondary education.[9] The report, which became known as *Investment in Education*, was finally published in 1965 and indicated that in the future education would form a major aspect of government economic policy.[10]

The findings of *Investment in Education* were to have a major impact on educational provision. In 1966, a number of reforms were implemented by the Department of Education, which transformed the existing system and had a direct impact on private boarding schools such as Kylemore Abbey. Firstly, the Department of Education announced its intention to provide free post-primary education up to Intermediate Certificate from September 1967. The new 'free education scheme' reduced the demand for fee-charging schools, especially once many private schools agreed to become 'free' by opting into the scheme, which gave supports to participating schools. Further, the Minister for Education announced a system of free school transport 'for all students residing at least three

Tree planting at Kylemore, from left to right: Sr Josephine O'Mahony, Sr John O'Malley, Sr Benedict O'Beirne, Dame (Sr) Margaret Mary Powell.

miles from a centre in which free post-primary education is available'.[11] By early June 1967, the free education scheme had been widely welcomed and accepted by 485 out of 595 secondary schools in the country.[12] Generally, the changes that came about had the effect of gradually making many boarding schools redundant, though the new policies did include provision for pupils who had no choice but to attend boarding school by 'making financial aid available to the pupil who because of his home location could have post-primary education available to him only if he entered a boarding school'.[13]

The impact of the free education scheme was immediate, resulting in a rise in pupil enrolments. In 1966–7 there was a total of 103,558 pupils enrolled in Irish secondary schools.[14] Following the introduction of free education, this figure rose to 118,807 students.[15] By 1972–3 the figure had reached 157,234 pupils.[16] The immediate rise in pupil numbers in September 1967 also affected staffing levels within the post-primary education system.

Table 5.1

Number of Teachers Employed in Secondary Schools, 1962–72

Year	No. of teachers employed	Increase on previous year
1962–3	5,908	278
1963–4	6,161	253
1964–5	6,477	316
1965–6	6,795	318
1966–7	7,248	453
1967–8	8,165	917
1972–3	11,250	NA

Source: Department of Education, *Annual Report*, 1962–72.

The growth in pupil and staff numbers in the secondary school sector coincided with a notable decline in the number of men and women entering religious life. This decline in religious vocations was to have a direct impact on staffing within the post-primary school system from the late 1960s onwards. Schools, including Kylemore, would need more lay teachers, especially to teach new subjects. The Department of Education made curricular reforms to incentivise the teaching of science – a subject in which few women religious in Ireland had been trained.

Classroom at Kylemore Abbey school.

From 1961 onwards, the Department of Education awarded grants for the establishment of science laboratories.[17] During the school year 1962/3, revised courses in chemistry and physics were also introduced.[18] Furthermore, from 1963 onwards, special financial incentives were awarded to school authorities for the employment of qualified science teachers.[19]

At Kylemore, the nuns had to embrace change as best they could. They also had to face a new reality: lay teachers were not only needed to respond to curricular changes, they were also needed because a noticeable fall in vocations to religious life had begun. Over a period of five years between 1965 and 1970, the number of religious teaching in the post-primary school sector in Ireland fell (see Table 5.2) and this was a pattern that would not be reversed. The causes for the decline in vocations were complex and were linked to changes generally in religious life following the Second Vatican Council.

This was a period of extraordinary change for the Benedictines of Kylemore Abbey, calling for resilience and for *Ora et Labora*.

Table 5.2 Number of Religious Teaching in the
Post-Primary School Sector, 1965–71

Year	Religious	Lay
1965–6	3,399 [50%]	3,396 [50%]
1967–8	3,690	4,475
1968–9	3,753	5,377
1969–70	3,703	5,900
1970–1	3,685 [34%]	6,548 [66%]

Source: *Education Times*, an *Irish Times* publication,
13 September 1973.

The Second Vatican Council and Religious Life in Ireland

In October 1962, Pope John XXIII formally opened the Second Ecumenical Council of the Vatican to consider relations between the Catholic Church and the modern world. The Council was closed under Pope Paul VI, on 8 December 1965. The deliberations of the Council resulted in many changes and adaptations in the Church and in religious life that had both an immediate and a long-term impact on communities of women religious and on convent schools such as Kylemore. One of the documents that directly concerned the lives of persons in religious orders, *Perfectae caritatis*, was subtitled 'Decree on the adaptation and renewal of religious life' and it called on religious to respond to the 'changed conditions of the times'.[20] Religious were asked to return to the sources and inspiration behind the foundation to which they belonged and to interpret the needs of contemporary society in light of the intent of their founders. In preparation for moving forward in the spirit of the Second Vatican Council, Mother Abbess Agnes attended seminars in England, joining with abbesses from other Benedictine houses for discussion and prayer.[21]

The Vatican Council left it to religious orders and institutes to determine the necessary changes and did not give rigid guidelines or instructions but it asked that religious respond to the conditions in which they worked. A number of operational changes took place in communities of women religious: most adopted a modified form of habit and women religious had the freedom to go outside the enclosure and could make visits home. The division of communities into choir and lay members was to be discontinued, though at Kylemore Abbey the contribution of lay sisters had already been recognised in 1960 when it was decided that sisters would be 'admitted to the Chapter with the right of active vote'.[22]

Perfectae caritatis recognised that communities entirely dedicated to contemplation lived their vocations differently from apostolic orders and noted that 'the exercises proper to the contemplative life should be preserved with the utmost care'.[23] Such orders were required, nonetheless, to suppress 'obsolete practices' and adapt their ancient traditions 'to the needs of today [so] that monasteries will become institutions dedicated to the edification of the Christian people'.[24]

For the Benedictines at Kylemore Abbey, the post-conciliar period did not bring dramatic change, because the community was already preserving the exercises proper to contemplative life, while also being manifestly dedicated to the edification of everyone with whom they came into contact – pupils, parents, teaching staff, farm workers, gardeners and the many Connemara neighbours who turned to the Abbey for prayer, support and education. There were a few changes that marked this new era in their Church: the nuns henceforth wore a slightly modified habit, with a simplified headdress; the vernacular was adopted in place of Latin for almost all of the Divine Office; the title 'Lady Abbess' was changed to 'Mother Abbess'; and the life of the Abbey continued.

In the Catholic Church, vocations to religious life were to wane in the decades after the Second Vatican Council. However, the Benedictines continued to welcome new members: two nuns were professed in the 1960s, three in the 1970s and four in the 1980s. The community also welcomed three members of the Benedictine community from Oulton Abbey, in England.

Developments at the Abbey and School

Though the community attracted vocations and the school was successful, the decades after the fire of 1959 demanded significant development so that the monastery and school remained viable. A number of projects were planned and executed with remarkable efficiency and success. The community decided to welcome more people to Kylemore by opening a pottery, shops and a tea room. They engaged successfully with Irish tourism, with support from Bord Tráchtála and Bord Fáilte, to make Kylemore Abbey an attractive and welcoming tourist destination, so that people could share the centuries of natural beauty and pray with the nuns. In the 1970s, the Office of Public Works (OPW) approached the community and asked them to sell part of the vast estate: the OPW purchased one thousand acres and created Connemara National Park. In the 1990s, the community joined the Rural Environmental Protection

---

Facing page, from top:

Sr Noreen (Peter) Gallagher with pupils, c.1970.

Addergoole Farm, Kylemore.

Sr Karol O'Connell working in the pottery, 1980s.

Scheme, which supports the values that underpin the way Benedictine monasteries have always farmed: environmentally friendly agricultural practices and traditional methods are supported and the natural habitat is conserved.

Alongside developments on the land, there were many initiatives needed in order to keep the abbey in repair: dry rot was found in the walls and the roof developed several leaks, so it was decided to try to restore parts of the estate that could be opened to the public, to bring in an income. Throughout the 1990s, the Benedictines developed an ambitious plan which resulted in the restoration of the walled gardens and the Gothic Church and the completion of badly needed repairs to the abbey. Tourists flocked to enjoy the unique beauty of Kylemore and the expanded tea rooms and craft shop that promoted local goods.

The New Millennium: A Legacy Continues

Though the 'Irish Dames of Ypres' weathered many challenges and changes after leaving Belgium during the First World War, the core of the monastic life of this community has remained unchanged: at intervals throughout the day, the nuns meet in chapel to mark the day by sung prayer. The daily prayer pattern, of matins, lauds, midday office, vespers and compline, is not an inward-looking activity, rather it embraces the whole world. It also vivifies the daily routines of monastic life. As one nun reflected, 'It's what gets you up in the morning and keeps you going throughout the day.'[25] Through the seasons, and across the closing decades of the twentieth century, sung prayer continued to unite the community on busy days that included teaching in the school and overseeing the work of the estate.

During those last decades of the century, some of the changes taking place outside the grounds of Kylemore began to have an impact on the school. The popularity of free secondary education and the provision of a state-supported school transport scheme meant that fewer families needed to send their children to boarding schools. Falling pupil numbers were not the only challenge to convent boarding schools: the fall in vocations to religious life meant that there was no longer a ready supply of nuns available around the clock to supervise full-time boarders.

Almost all Catholic boarding schools would close their doors for good by the early twenty-first century. Kylemore Abbey school closed in 2010, by which time, of a staff of twenty-three, only one teacher was a member of the Benedictine community.

However, teaching was not the only labour of the nuns; they have continued to work in other areas of local and national importance. They run a small soap factory and a chocolate factory on the estate, making products to sell in the shop. They are involved in music education and teacher education, attracting teachers from around the country to summer courses. And they remain a central support to their

Below: Sr Benedict O'Beirne driving the cows at Addergoole Farm, 1980s.
Facing page: President Mary Robinson with Abbess Clare Morley and schoolchildren at the reopening of the Gothic Church, 1995.

local community, as the biggest employer in Connemara. They have cultivated the sense of community that was established in the nineteenth century by Mitchell Henry, employing generations of families and living alongside them on the estate. And they have embedded in Kylemore the values of St Benedict that were first articulated in the sixth century.

A call to monastic life is, above all, a call to a certain type of prayer.[26] The nuns in Kylemore today agree that they were attracted to Benedictine life because, at its centre, is sung prayer.[27] The work of a monastery can vary according to local needs and demands, but the prayer is constant. In the words of one nun: 'As I get older, and contemplate the last judgment, I can say, I have sung in choir, praising God with the angels.'[28]

The history of the Order of St Benedict has not been without its setbacks. Within fifty years of St Benedict's death, Monte Cassino was destroyed in the Lombard invasions, as were most other monasteries in central Italy. Indeed, throughout Europe, there were centuries during which monasteries were suppressed. The complete suppression of the monasteries in England by 1539 did not bode well for Benedictine houses, yet many of them survived and managed to restore themselves and flourish again. The history of the Irish Dames of Ypres is just one example of how nuns have survived great setbacks.

Benedictines have always recognised the importance of *Ora et Labora* in this kind of survival, adaptation and growth. They are also sustained by the second Benedictine motto, *Pax*, to which they often refer. Mother Abbess Máire reminds us of a third – and less frequently quoted – Benedictine motto: *succisa virescit* (Job 14:7), which can be translated as, 'the cut-down tree greens again'.[29]

Facing page: Sr Benedict O'Beirne making butter.
Overleaf: Sr Genevieve Harrington, *c*.2000.

Clockwise from left:
Sr Benedict O'Beirne,
Sr Aidan Ryan,
Sr Magdalena FitzGibbon,
Sr Genevieve Harrington, 2000.

Sr Josephine O'Mahony,
Sr Benedict O'Beirne,
Sr Karol O'Connell,
Sr Genevieve Harrigton, 2000.

Lace-making.

Facing page: Abbess Magdalena FitzGibbon (2001–6).
Above: Sr Benedict O'Beirne at Addergoole Farm.

'Whenever you begin any good work,
you should first of all make a most
pressing appeal to Christ our Lord
to bring it to perfection.'

St Benedict (AD 480–547)

EPILOGUE

For there is hope for a tree, if it be cut down, that it will
sprout again, and that its shoots will not cease. (Job 14:7)

The preceding chapters told a story of a group of Irish Catholic
women who formed a Benedictine community 350 years ago.
The women came and went as members of the community, lived
and died, and their places were taken by women of the following
generation, in Dublin, in Ypres, in County Wexford and then, since
1920, in Kylemore, Connemara. The community throve, declined,
struggled and recovered again many times. The final chapter shows our
community of ten nuns on the eve of our celebration of one hundred
years in Kylemore.

Underlying the history of the Benedictine nuns of Ypres from 1665
until the present day in Kylemore is a universal story about the resilience
of human beings and the sustainability of the human condition. It is a
tale of hope, courage, resourcefulness and the will to survive in the face
of the most threatening adversity. There are many such stories. Some
of them – by no means all – have a religious background: the actors in
these stories know they are connected with a power beyond their ken,
whose presence plays a deciding role in giving meaning to their lives and

survival. They are carried along by an awareness of God as a powerful force, whose ultimate benevolence is totally reliable despite the terrible afflictions that he appears to allow. Such faith, and the desire to share it with others, brought the Benedictine nuns first to Ypres then eventually to Kylemore. It is at the heart of the teaching of Jesus and the message of the Christian Church. It is the faith of St Benedict of Nursia, whose Rule was an inspirational factor in the survival of our civilisation until the present time. It is summed up in the motto of the first Abbess of Kylemore, Dame Mary Maura Ostyn, taken from the Psalter that was and remains the substance of the daily prayer of Benedictine monks and nuns:

Commit your way to the Lord. Trust in him. He will act.
(Psalm 37:5)

Kylemore as visitors experience it today has developed, following the lead of Abbess Ostyn, from the beautiful Victorian home of a wealthy family into a modern monastic community. The ten Benedictine nuns who currently reside here are continuing the tradition of living in community, sharing our liturgy and hospitality in a spirit of peace with all. Our stated goal is to keep the estate open for the education and enjoyment of everyone who visits, and for the common good of Connemara.

However, we do not have an appropriate monastic building in which to live together according to the Rule, and to train new members in the monastic way of community living. We have lived for over ten years in temporary quarters in the nineteenth-century farm building on the Kylemore estate. After ninety years of sharing their space in the castle with a girls' boarding school and a growing tourist business, the community decided on a ten-year development plan that would include a new, purpose-built monastery. The plan also encompasses long-overdue repair and conservation works on the castle, and ongoing restoration of the Victorian walled garden, the Gothic Church and the estate, to make Kylemore sustainable for its future as a visitor destination and a support to the economy of the region.

We have often been asked, 'Does twenty-first-century Ireland need a new monastery at Kylemore or, indeed, anywhere?' Moving daily among the half a million visitors who pass through Kylemore every year, greeting them and engaging in conversation, we are encountering a cross-section of the burdens of modern life. People are hungry for the healing the human spirit needs when it is wounded through broken relationships, homelessness and abuse. Rampant materialism and social chaos are wreaking havoc on lives and families. Many visitors express profound gratitude for Kylemore's tranquillity and sense of peace, which draws their spirits away from the stress and brutality of the age of technology. Kylemore, with its stunningly beautiful atmosphere and the insight it offers into a contemplative way of life, is somewhere people can find a hint of direction and meaning for their personal journeys.

As the Catholic Church in Ireland works through radical changes in society, and Ireland reaches out to find its place among the nations of the earth in the twenty-first century, our community recognises that many elements of monastic life that characterised our existence at Kylemore since 1920 are no longer adequate to today's mission. The Rule, and the great family of men and women who have committed their lives to following it, survives because of its truth and adaptability to changing circumstances. In keeping with this, the new monastery will focus its spirituality (preferring nothing to Christ) and its practice of hospitality (finding Christ in the stranger) on engagement with new times and with people burdened with the challenges of those new times. If a monastic community can adapt its outreach to contemporary life in order to serve some of these basic human needs, then, unquestionably, Kylemore is a godsend.

Our new monastery building will enhance the spiritual life of our community and provide an environment in which newcomers can grow into the contemplative practices of silence, prayerful order, liturgy, study, work, and balanced community living.

Our enclosure is not exclusive. The contemplative core of the new monastery will be surrounded by the vibrantly humming life of the estate, with all its apparatus of administration, management, production, services operated by teams of dedicated staff and volunteers as well as the thousands of visitors coming and going every day. There will be new guest rooms for residential retreats, spacious reception areas for larger groups and events, and intimate spaces for one-to-one meetings and small groups. The facilities offered by our strategic partnership with the University of Notre Dame global centre at Kylemore and our own catering facilities will enable us to host educational activities, cultural events and conferences reflecting on burning issues of the day. Contemplative ecology will be a hallmark of our programme for sustainability in every area of life at Kylemore. Work on the first phase of the new monastery started in October 2019, and is scheduled to be completed by November 2020, in time to celebrate the arrival of the nuns from Ypres in December 1920.

The preparation for our centenary celebrations is an appropriate occasion for us to offer our thanks to all those who have, during the past hundred years, supported us through their goodwill and friendship. Countless individuals have encouraged us with their appreciation for our way of life and by sharing our vision for a new monastery. The cut-down tree could never have sprouted again without the ongoing help of the large extended Benedictine family that has grown around our community. It began with the monks of Maredsous/Edermine (later Glenstal) who pointed the way to our future home after we had left Ypres, and to the County Wexford families who provided a haven of welcome and remain our faithful friends to this day. The Archdiocese of Tuam and the people of Connemara gave us a place in their midst where we could put down roots, grow, and carry out our mission. A special word of thanks must go to our US friends whose enthusiasm and unfailing commitment from the 1990s onwards energised us to launch the then programme for the restoration of Kylemore, and to persevere with it through thick and thin. In recent times, newer friends of outstanding generosity have helped us with significant philanthropy, others through volunteer work, professional competence, fundraising, gifts in kind, and innumerable gestures of kindness and solidarity. Our warm thanks too to the alumnae of Kylemore Abbey School, who act as our ambassadors all around the world and never fail to go the extra mile when Kylemore needs them.

We draw all of our friends and supporters into our daily prayer here at the Abbey, and look forward to welcoming them soon to our new monastery at the heart of Kylemore.

God bless you all.
Abbess Máire Hickey OSB

ENDNOTES

Chapter One
THE IRISH DAMES OF YPRES

1   Laurence Lux-Sterritt, *English Benedictine Nuns in Exile in the Seventeenth Century* (Manchester: Manchester University Press, 2017), p. 129.

2   Scholars writing about Benedictine women and their foundations use the terms 'monastery' and 'convent' interchangeably.

3   Stephanus Hilpisch OSB, *History of Benedictine Nuns* (Minnesota: St John's Abbey Press, 1958), p. 14.

4   Ibid., p. 15.

5   Ibid., p. 22.

6   Ibid., pp. 42–3.

7   For an explanation, and exploration of *lectio divina*, see David Foster OSB, *Reading with God: Lectio Divina* (London and New York: Continuum International Publishing, 2005).

8   Ibid., p. 60.

9   Lux-Sterritt, *English Benedictine Nuns*, p. xvii. Lady Mary Percy was the daughter of Thomas Percy, Earl of Northumberland.

10 Ibid.

11 Kathleen Villiers-Tuthill, 'The Irish Benedictine Nuns: From Ypres to Kylemore' in Martin Browne OSB and Colmán Ó Clabaigh OSB, *The Irish Benedictines: A History* (Dublin: The Columba Press, 2005), p. 122.

12 In 1658, the foundation in Boulogne closed and its community transferred to Pontoise. See Patrick Nolan, *The Irish Dames of Ypres, Being a History of the Royal Irish Abbey of Ypres Founded A.D. 1665 and Still Flourishing and Some Account of the Irish Jacobitism with a Portrait of James II and Stuart Letters Hitherto Unpublished* (Dublin: Browne and Nolan Limited, 1908), p. 16.

13 Villiers-Tuthill, 'The Irish Benedictine Nuns', p. 123.

14 Among the first religious in Ypres were Dames Marina Beaumont (Superioress), Aloysia German, Aldegonde Finch, Mary Lucy and a lay sister, Sr Martha, all from the community in Ghent. They were joined in Ypres by Sr Jenison, a novice in Dunkirk. See Nolan, *The Irish Dames of Ypres*, p. 33.

15 Lux-Sterritt, *English Benedictine Nuns*, p. xx.

16 Within a year of their arrival in Ypres, the three Dames who had accompanied Abbess Beaumont returned to Ghent. Three novices who had been admitted at Ypres also left the community. As a result of an outbreak of plague in Dunkirk, three more Dames were sent to Ypres. However, they only remained

in the community for a few short years before returning to Dunkirk taking with them the lay sister, Sr Martha. See Nolan, *The Irish Dames of Ypres*, pp. 38–9.

17 It is not clear when Dame Flavia Carey joined the community in Ypres but according to the diary of Lady Abbess Neville (fourth Abbess of Pontoise), 'D. Flavia Carey [was] a most excellent Regular good Religious woman, that was sent to the new establishment at Dunkirk, and from thence summoned by my Lord Bishop Praets to assist my Lady Marina at Ypres. He being Superior both to Dunkirk and Ypres; she was obliged to obey, and was a great support to my Lady Marina …' Diary of Lady Abbess Neville cited in Nolan, *The Irish Dames of Ypres*, pp. 39–40.

18 Ibid., p. 41.

19 Ibid.

20 Ibid., pp. 41–2.

21 MS Annals of the Benedictine Abbey, Ypres, cited in Nolan, *The Irish Dames of Ypres*, pp. 52–3.

22 Ibid., p. 53.

23 It is possible that the reference to Rev. Dame Mary Joseph O'Bryan from Dunkirk is a misprint and that the Dame in question was actually Mary Joseph Ryan who, having failed to establish an Irish Benedictine foundation in Dunkirk, was sent to Ypres c.1682. See MS Annals of the Benedictine Abbey, Ypres, cited in Nolan, *The Irish Dames of Ypres*, pp. 53–4.

24 Ibid.

25 Dame Ryan was accompanied by Dame Ursula Butler. Dame Butler did not return to Ypres but travelled to England for the coronation of King James II. She died in England soon after. See Villiers-Tuthill, 'The Irish Benedictine Nuns', p. 124.

26 According to Nolan, Dame Ryan had returned to Ireland in 1685 to procure 'pupils and subjects and money for Ypres'. See Nolan, *The Irish Dames of Ypres*, p. 174.

27 Villiers-Tuthill, 'The Irish Benedictine Nuns', p. 124.

28 Mrs Thomas Concannon, *Irish Nuns in Penal Days* (Rochester and Kent: The Standhope Press Limited, 1931), p. 100.

29 King Moylan, 'The district of Grangegorman: part III' in *Dublin Historical Record*, 7:3 (June–August, 1945), p. 105.

30 According to Concannon, Dame Ryan also obtained 'authorisation of her Abbess in Dunkirk' to establish the foundation in Dublin. See Concannon, *Irish Nuns in Penal Days*, p. 97.

31 See Lux-Sterritt, *English Benedictine Nuns*, p. 128.

32 Ibid.

33 Moylan, 'The district of Grangegorman: part III', p. 105.

34 W.O. Cavenagh, 'The Irish Benedictine nunnery at Ypres, Belgium', *The Journal of the Royal Society of Antiquaries of Ireland*, Fifth Series, 38:2 (June 30, 1908), pp. 179–80.

35 Villiers-Tuthill, 'The Irish Benedictine

Nuns', p. 125.

36 Dame Neville died from an accident on her way to Ireland on 25 September 1687. See Fr Brocard Mansfield, 'A short-lived Royal Dublin foundation' *Dublin Historical Record*, 36:2 (Mar, 1983), p. 65.

37 Ibid.

38 Ibid.

39 Villiers-Tuthill, 'The Irish Benedictine Nuns', p. 126.

40 Mansfield, 'A short-lived Royal Dublin foundation', pp. 65–7.

41 Concannon, *Irish Nuns in Penal Days*, pp. 101–3.

42 MS Annals of the Benedictine Abbey, Ypres, cited in Nolan, *The Irish Dames of Ypres*, pp. 208–9.

43 Ibid., p. 209.

44 Ibid.

45 Nolan, *The Irish Dames of Ypres*, p. 210.

46 Villiers-Tuthill, 'The Irish Benedictine Nuns', pp. 127–9.

47 See Deirdre Raftery, Catriona Delaney and Catherine Nowlan-Roebuck, *Nano Nagle, The Life and the Legacy* (Kildare: Irish Academic Press, 2019), p. 20.

48 Abbess Lynch to Teresa Mulally, 24 February 1784, George's Hill Archives Dublin (hereafter GHAD), IE PBVM [GHD] 3, A.I (i) FD/12; Abbess Lynch to Teresa Mulally, 13 August 1784, GHAD, IE PBVM [GHD] 3, A.I (i) FD/13.

49 Villiers-Tuthill, 'The Irish Benedictine Nuns', p. 129.

50 Ibid.

51 Nolan, *The Irish Dames of Ypres*, pp.

330–1.

52 Ibid., pp. 332–3.

53 See Deirdre Raftery, 'Rebels with a cause: obedience, resistance and convent life, 1800–1940', *History of Education*, 42:6 (2013), pp. 729–44.

Chapter Two
THE JOURNEY TOWARDS KYLEMORE, 1914–1920

1   See J. Sheldon, *The German Army at Ypres 1914* (London: Pen & Sword Military, 2010).

2   Ypres Diary 1914 –, KAA1/1. It was to be ten years before three of the German nuns rejoined their community in Kylemore; one nun had died in Holland.

3   Dame M. Columban Plomer OSB (Member of the Community), *The Irish Nuns at Ypres: An Episode of the War* (London: Smith, Elder & Co., 1915), p. 3.

4   Ibid.

5   John Redmond MP in Introduction to Plomer, *The Irish Nuns at Ypres*, p. xvi.

6   Plomer, *The Irish Nuns at Ypres*, p. 2.

7   Ibid.

8   Henry V. Gill, 'The Fate of the Irish Flag at Ypres', *Studies, An Irish Quarterly Review*, 8:29 (March, 1919), p. 120.

9   Plomer, *The Irish Nuns at* Ypres, p. 25.

10 Loose-leaf MS diary of WWI departure from Ypres, p. 53, KAA1/1.

11 See Sheldon, *The German Army at Ypres 1914*.

12 Loose-leaf MS diary of WWI departure from Ypres, p. 61, KAA1/1.

13 MS notebook, Oulton to Highfield, p. 72, KAA1/1.

14 Ibid.

15 Ibid., p. 75.

16 Villiers-Tuthill, 'The Irish Benedictine Nuns', pp. 133–4. John Redmond (1856–1918) leader of the Irish Parliamentary Party from 1900 until his death. His niece was Mother Teresa Howard OSB.

17 Gill, 'The Fate of the Irish Flag at Ypres', p. 121.

18 Ibid., p. 122.

19 Ibid.

20 Ypres Diary, 1914– , KAA1/1.

21 Diary of Dame Teresa Howard, p. 5, KAA/1/1.

22 This notebook contains, in addition to her recipes, lots of other information which might prove useful to the nuns, including a cure for rheumatism: 'A little powdered sulphur worn in the foot of each stocking for a few days then replaced by fresh is in many cases a cure for rheumatism and it has the merit of being an inexpensive remedy', KAA, uncatalogued.

23 MS loose-leaf diary on WWI departure from Ypres, p. 62, KAA/1/1.

24 Ibid., p. 63.

25 Ibid.

26 Ibid.

27 Register, 'Pupils educated at the Ypres Benedictine Abbey: Merton 1916', is the roll book from 1916 in Merton until 1924 in Kylemore Abbey, KAA2/1/2,

No. 2.

28 See Ida Milne, *Stacking the Coffins: Influenza, War and Revolution in Ireland 1918–1919* (Manchester: Manchester University Press, 2018).

29 *The* [Wexford] *People*, 23 August 1916, p. 4.

30 'Account of the Purchase of Kylemore Castle and Estate, now Kylemore Abbey OSB', p. 1, KAA1/4, No. 2.

31 MS document, untitled, KAA1/4, No. 2.

32 'Account of the Purchase of Kylemore Castle and Estate, now Kylemore Abbey OSB', p. 1, KAA1/4, No. 2.

33 Ibid.

34 Ibid.

35 MS document, untitled, KAA1/1, uncatalogued.

36 Ibid.

37 Ibid.

38 Ibid.

39 Ibid.

40 Ibid.

Chapter Three
CONNEMARA AND KYLEMORE IN THE NINETEENTH CENTURY

1 E.Oe. Somerville and V.M. Ross, *Through Connemara in a Governess Cart* (London: W.H. Allen, 1893), p. 118.

2 For a discussion of the English convents, see Caroline Bowden (ed.), *English Convents in Exile 1600–1800*, 6 vols (London: Pickering & Chatto, 2011–2013).

3   Maeve Mulryan Moloney, *Nineteenth-Century Elementary Education in the Archdiocese of Tuam* (Dublin and Portland OR: Irish Academic Press, 2001), p. 7.

4   Eibhlín Ni Scannláin, *Land and the People: Land Uses and Population Change in North and West Connemara in the 19th Century* (Connemara: Connemara West plc and Dúchas, the Heritage Service, 1999), p. 62.

5   Mulryan Moloney, *Nineteenth-Century Elementary Education*, p. 1.

6   For a discussion of education in the deanery of Clifden, see Kieran Waldron, *Out of the Shadows, Emerging Secondary Schools in the Archdiocese of Tuam, 1940–69* (Tuam: Nordlaw Books, 2002), pp. 71–3, *passim.*

7   Ibid., pp. 55–7.

8   Ibid., p. 9.

9   In October 1831, Lord Stanley, the Chief Secretary to Ireland, wrote to the Lord Lieutenant outlining the government plan regarding a system of national education for Ireland. This became known as the Stanley Letter. The main aims of the proposed system were to afford 'a combined literary and separate religious education ... for the poorer classes of the community' and 'to unite in one system children of different creeds'. The Stanley Letter, in *Royal Commission of Inquiry into Primary Education (Ireland), Vol. I, Pt. I: Report of the Commissioners; with an appendix*, pt. i.: 22–6. The new system was overseen by the Commissioners for National Education in Ireland (CNEI).

10   See Mulryan Moloney, *Nineteenth-Century Elementary Education.*

11   Mulryan Moloney, *Nineteenth-Century Elementary Education*, p. 35.

12   James Hack Tuke (1819–96) was an English Quaker, who came to Ireland in 1846–7 to distribute relief on behalf of the Society of Friends. He served on the Congested Districts Board from 1891–4. In 1882, he established the 'Tuke Committee', a group of wealthy Englishmen, to raise funds to assist Irish families to emigrate from the West of Ireland. The use of assisted emigration as a 'solution' to the consequences of poverty, crop failure and eviction has been critiqued by many scholars. For a study of assisted emigration see Gerard Moran, *Sending Out Ireland's Poor: Assisted Emigration to North America in the Nineteenth Century* (Dublin: Four Courts Press, 2013). For an overview of Tuke's schemes, see Gerard Moran, 'James Hack Tuke and his schemes for assisted emigration from the West of Ireland', *History Ireland*, May/June 2013, pp. 30–3. See David Fitzpatrick, *Irish Emigration, 1801–1921* (Dundalk: Economic and Social History Society of Ireland, 1984), p. 19; see also Ni Scannláin, *Land and the People*, p. 68.

13   Kathleen Villiers-Tuthill, *History of Kylemore Castle & Abbey* (Kylemore Abbey: Kylemore Abbey Publications, 2002; reprinted 2013), p. 4.

14   'Catalogue for the Sale of Kylemore Castle' (1902), 8–10, KAA1/8/1, No. 40.

15 Ibid., pp. 16–17.

16 See Ellen M. Blake, *My Connemara Childhood* (Limerick: Ashford Press, 1999), p. 23. Blake was a playmate of the Henry children and visited the castle; she recalled the abundance of oranges, bananas and pineapples, grown in the glasshouses on the estate, and the pleasure of roaming in the gardens, picking fruit. For a description of Kylemore Castle and the range of outbuildings and glasshouses, see 'Catalogue for the Sale of Kylemore Castle' (1902), KAA1/8/1, No. 40.

17 'Catalogue for the Sale of Kylemore Castle' (1902), KAA1/8/1, No. 40, p. 19.

18 Ibid., pp. 20–1.

19 *The Freeman's Journal*, 4 March 1871.

20 For a detailed account of the development of Kylemore under the Henrys, see Villiers-Tuthill, *History of Kylemore*.

21 Hansard's Parliamentary Debates vol ccxii 1872, 1783–1799. M. Henry. Cited in Villiers-Tuthill, *History of Kylemore*, p. 64.

22 Extracts from Hansard's Parliamentary Debates, Vol. CCXL, KAA/10/6, External Documents.

23 Extracts from Hansard's Parliamentary Debates, Vol. CCXIV, KAA/10/6, External Documents.

24 Villiers-Tuthill, *History of Kylemore*, p. 19.

25 See Mulryan Moloney, *Nineteenth-Century Elementary Education*, p. 34.

26 Amelia Edwards, *A Thousand Miles Up the Nile* (London: Routledge and Sons, 1888), pp. 4–6.

27 It is unclear exactly how Mitchell Henry brought the body of Margaret Henry back to Ireland, though Villiers-Tuthill suggests that the embalmed body may have been kept with the family in Egypt while they remained there through the winter and into the spring. In 1882, a small gothic chapel and burial place was built in her memory at Kylemore and her remains were reinterred there.

28 Ni Scannláin, *Land and the People*, p. 66.

29 *Galway Vindicator*, 10 September 1879, p. 3, cited in Villiers-Tuthill, p. 89.

30 For a description of life at Kylemore, and of the members of the Henry family, see Villiers-Tuthill, *History of Kylemore*, chapter 9, *passim*.

31 Ibid., p. 128.

32 'Catalogue for the Sale of Kylemore Castle' (1902), KAA1/8/1, No. 40.

33 Ibid., pp. 1–3.

34 Ibid., p. 1.

35 The Duke of Manchester, *My Candid Recollections* (London, 1932), p. 209, cited in Villiers-Tuthill, *History of Kylemore*, p. 139.

36 Edward VII had called to the castle in 1903, see Villiers-Tuthill, *History of Kylemore*, p. 129.

37 See Villiers-Tuthill, *History of Kylemore*, p. 137.

38 Ibid., p. 143.

Chapter Four

THE BENEDICTINES AT
KYLEMORE ABBEY, 1920–1959

1   'Pupils educated at the Ypres
     Benedictine Abbey: Merton 1916',
     KAA2/1/2, No. 2.
2   MS Necrology, Kylemore Abbey,
     uncatalogued.
3   Nola McD to Dame Scholastica, 14
     January 1925, KAA2/1/1, No. 1.
4   Vivian Clodagh Moore to Dame
     Scholastica, 17 February 1925,
     KAA2/1/1, No. 1.
5   'Pupils educated at the Ypres
     Benedictine Abbey: Merton 1916',
     KAA2/1/2, No. 2. However, the official
     opening date is given as 11 September
     1923, when thirty pupils were enrolled.
6   Ibid.
7   Enrolments in 1921–2 included:
     Shirley (12) and Muriel (18) Robinson,
     England; Anne (12) and Margaret (17)
     Hartigan, Limerick; Ursula Glynn (12),
     Galway; Kathleen Brooks (14), Tuam;
     Nora O'Connor (14), Navan; Caroline
     McNally (14), Kells; Beulah Stracham
     (17), Tuam; Rosaline (8), Veronica
     (10) and Winnie (12) Flinn, Dublin;
     Betty (10) and Doreen (12) Leonard,
     Waterford; Violet (15) and Pauline (17)
     Slattery, Limerick.
8   Kathleen Buckley to Dame Scholastica,
     23 December 1925, KAA2/1/1, No. 1.
9   E.M. Redmond, Danesfort, Clontarf,
     Co. Dublin to Dame Scholastica, 23
     December 1925, KAA2/1/1, No. 1.
10   Philip O'Gorman to Dame Scholastica,

15 Dec 1925, KAA2/1/1, No. 1.
11   Department of Education, Report of
     the Inspector, Kylemore Abbey 1924–
     5, KAA, uncatalogued.
12   *Department of Education Statistical
     Report, 1925–26–27* (Dublin, 1927),
     pp. 152–3 and 133.
13   Brother Paul Hogan CBS to Rev Fr
     [unknown], 31 July 1928, [Letter
     sends greetings to Dame Scholastica.],
     KAA2/1/1, No. 2.
14   Irene O'Callaghan to Dame Scholastica,
     5 Jan 1926, KAA2/1/1, No. 1.
15   Thomas H. Weaving to Dame
     Scholastica, 10 March 1925, KAA2/1/1,
     No. 1.
16   Thomas H. Weaving to Dame
     Scholastica, 2 April 1925, KAA2/1/1,
     No. 1.
17   Frances Mulligan to Dame Scholastica,
     16 October 1926, KAA2/1/1, No. 1.
     The other past pupil commenced a
     Law degree at Trinity College Dublin
     in 1927. See Frances Mulligan to
     Dame Scholastica, 8 February 1927,
     KAA2/1/1, No. 1.
18   House Annals 1940–57, KAA1/2/3,
     No. 1.
19   Ibid.
20   Ibid.
21   Council Meetings, 1929–46, 20 August
     1929, Kylemore Abbey, uncatalogued.
22   Villiers-Tuthill, *History of Kylemore*, p.
     183.
23   Council Minutes, 1929–46, Meeting
     of the Chapter, 2 November 1929,
     Kylemore Abbey, uncatalogued.
24   House Annals 1940–57, KAA1/2/3,

No. 1.

25 Council Minutes, 1952–78, 6 August 1953, Kylemore Abbey, uncatalogued.

26 Council Minutes, 1952–78, 1 July 1952, Kylemore Abbey, uncatalogued.

27 Council Minutes, 1952–78, 22 July 1952.

28 Council Minutes, 1952–78, 21 August 1952.

29 Council Minutes, 1952–78, 16 December 1954.

30 See, for example, Council Minutes, 1952–78, 4 June 1971.

31 Council Minutes, 1952–7, 30 December 1952.

32 TS interview with Teresa Lydon, 10 March 1998, KAA1/10/6, No. 1.

33 Ibid.

34 'A synopsis of the life of Sr Benedict O'Beirne OSB', Synopsis 8, KAA, uncatalogued.

35 Ibid.

36 Ibid.

37 Ibid., Synopsis 9.

38 Sr Benedict O'Beirne, Archivist, in Dame Magdalen Lee OSB, *By Strange Paths* (Kylemore: Kylemore Abbey Publications, 2002), pp. 70–1.

39 Ibid.

40 Ibid.

41 'A Synopsis of the life of Sr Benedict O'Beirne OSB', Synopsis 8, KAA, uncatalogued.

42 Ibid., p. 26.

43 Ibid., p. 34.

44 House Annals 1940–57, KAA1/2/3, No. 1.

45 Necrology, Lady Abbess Mary Placid Druhan OSB. Kylemore Abbey, uncatalogued.

46 Department of Education, *Annual Report*, 1960–1 (Dublin: 1961), pp. 126 and 134. Hereafter DE, *Annual Report*. In addition to the recognised secondary and secondary top schools, there were also vocational or 'continuation' schools. However, pupils attending these schools were not permitted to sit the Intermediate or Leaving Certificate examinations until the late 1960s. See John Logan, 'All the children: the vocational school and education reform 1930–90' in John Logan (ed.), *Teachers' Union, the TUI and its Forerunners, 1899–1994* (Dublin: A&A Farmar, 1999), pp. 277–89.

47 In 1958, a year before the fire that destroyed most of the Kylemore school, the average income per family working in the agricultural sector was £288.60 while the average income per family working in the non-agricultural sector was £379. See Kieran A. Kennedy and Richard Bruton, 'The Irish economy', in *Economic and Financial Series*, 10 (1975), p. 40.

48 During the eighteenth and nineteenth centuries, religious institutions tended to develop in economically affluent regions where there was a prosperous Catholic population willing and able to support religious orders and their works of charity. See Paula Coonerty, 'The Presentation Sisters and the education of "poor female children" in Limerick, 1837–1870', *The Old Limerick Journal*

(Winter 1996), p. 37.

49 Department of Education, *Data on Individual Secondary Schools*, 1962–3.

Chapter Five

GROWTH AND CHANGE AT KYLEMORE ABBEY, 1959–2019

1 For a full description of the fire and the days that followed, see Villiers-Tuthill, *History of Kylemore*, pp. 199–206.

2 Ibid.

3 Mother Mechtilde Moloney in conversation with Kathleen Villiers-Tuthill, July 2000. Cited in Villiers-Tuthill, *History of Kylemore*, p. 202.

4 Chapter Affairs, 1935–2008, 15 February 1959 and 1 May 1959, Kylemore Abbey, uncatalogued.

5 Department of Education, *Annual Report*, 1940–1, p. 94.

6 Department of Education, *Annual Report*, 1958–9, p. 79 and 1964–5, p. 39.

7 John Coolahan, *Irish Education, History and Structure* (Dublin: Institute of Public Administration, 1981), p. 131.

8 The two Irish delegates were Seán MacGearailt and John F. McInerney. See John Walsh, *The Politics of Expansion: The Transformation of Educational Policy in the Republic of Ireland, 1957–72* (Manchester: Manchester University Press, 2009), p. 64.

9 The survey team appointed by Hillery consisted of Patrick Lynch, lecturer in economics at University College,

Dublin; William J. Hyland, of the Statistics Office, United Nations; Martin O'Donoghue, lecturer in economics at Trinity College, Dublin, and Pádraig Uasal Ó Nualláin, inspector of secondary schools. Cathal Uasal Mac Gabhann of the Department of Education was appointed Secretary. See Department of Education, *Report of the Survey Team Appointed by the Minister for Education, Investment in Education, Ireland* (Dublin, 1965), p. XXXVII. Hereafter, *Investment in Education*.

10 *Investment in Education*, p. 31.

11 Department of Education, circular m. 15/67, February 1967.

12 Department of Education, *Annual Report*, 1967–8.

13 See Eileen Randles, *Post-Primary Education in Ireland, 1957–70* (Dublin: Veritas, 1975), pp. 218–19.

14 Department of Education, *Annual Report*, 1966–7.

15 Department of Education, *Annual Report*, 1967–8.

16 Department of Education, *Annual Report*, 1973.

17 Walsh, *The Politics of Expansion*, p. 76.

18 Department of Education, *Annual Report*, 1962–3, p. 58.

19 In September 1963, the Department of Education announced that 'an additional science grant (teaching grant) amounting to £150 per annum is payable under certain conditions to secondary schools in respect of each graduate science teacher on the staff'. See Department of Education, *Progress*

Report for quarter ended 7th September 1963. National Archives of Ireland, TSCH/3/S 15064 C/63.

20 *Perfectae caritatis. Decree on the adaptation and renewal of religious life.* Proclaimed by His Holiness Pope Paul VI, 28 October 1965.

21 Miscellaneous papers, KAA, uncata-logued.

22 Chapter Affairs, 1935–2008, 17 January 1960, Kylemore Abbey, uncatalogued.

23 *Perfectae caritatis*, § 7.

24 *Perfectae caritatis*, § 9.

25 Kylemore Abbey community member, in conversation with the authors, May 2019.

26 Cyprian Smith OSB, *The Path of Life* (York: Ampleforth Abbey Press, 1995; reprinted 1996 & 2004), p. 122.

27 The Kylemore Abbey community in conversation with the authors, May 2019.

28 Kylemore Abbey community member, in conversation with the authors, May 2019.

29 Mother Abbess Máire Hickey, in conversation with the authors, May 2019.

BIBLIOGRAPHY

I. MANUSCRIPT SOURCES

Kylemore Abbey Archives

Ypres Diary, 1914–
    Loose-leaf diary of WWI departure
    from Ypres
Notebook, Oulton to Highfield
House Annals [Kylemore Abbey] 1940–57
Diary of Dame Teresa Howard
Register, Pupils educated at the Ypres
    Benedictine Abbey: Merton 1916
Account of the Purchase of Kylemore Castle
    and Estate, now Kylemore Abbey OSB
Miscellaneous Papers, untitled
Letters to Dame Scholastica Murphy
Synopsis of the life of Sr Benedict O'Beirne

Kylemore Abbey, Community Papers

Council Meetings [Minutes], 1929–46
Council Minutes, 1952–78
Chapter Affairs [Minutes], 1935–2008
Necrologia
Miscellaneous Papers

**Presentation Sisters Archives, George's
    Hill, Dublin**

Letters of Abbess Lynch to Theresa Mulally

II. PUBLISHED PRIMARY SOURCES

Catalogue for the Sale of Kylemore Castle,
    1902.
Nolan, Patrick OSB, *The Irish Dames of
    Ypres, being a history of the Royal Irish
    Abbey of Ypres founded A.D. 1665 and*
*still flourishing and some account of the
    Irish Jacobitism with a portrait of James
    II and Stuart letters hitherto unpublished*
    (Dublin: Browne and Nolan Limited,
    1908).
Plomer, Dame Columban OSB (Member
    of the Community), *The Irish Nuns at
    Ypres: An Episode of the War* (London:
    Smith, Elder & Co., 1915).
Somerville, E. Oe. and Ross, V.M., *Through
    Connemara in a Governess Cart*
    (London: W.H. Allen, 1893).

III. OFFICIAL PUBLICATIONS

Department of Education, *Annual Report*,
    1940–1.
Department of Education, *Annual Report*,
    1958–9.
Department of Education, *Annual Report*,
    1960–1.
Department of Education, *Annual Report*,
    1962–3.
Department of Education, *Annual Report*,
    1964–5.
Department of Education, *Annual Report*,
    1966–7.
Department of Education, *Annual Report*,
    1967–8.
Department of Education, circular m.
    15/67, February 1967.
Department of Education, *Annual Report*,
    1973.
Department of Education, *Data on*

Individual Secondary Schools, 1962–3.

Department of Education, *Progress Report for quarter ended 7th September 1963*.

Department of Education, *Report of the Survey Team Appointed by the Minister for Education, Investment in Education, Ireland* (Dublin: 1965).

IV. VATICAN PUBLICATIONS

Perfectae caritatis. Decree on the adaptation and renewal of religious life.

Proclaimed by His Holiness Pope Paul VI, 28 October 1965.

V. BOOKS

Browne, Martin OSB and Ó Clabaigh, Colmán OSB, *The Irish Benedictines: A History* (Dublin: The Columba Press, 2005).

Concannon, Mrs Thomas, *Irish Nuns in Penal Days* (Edinburgh: Sands and Co., 1931).

Coolahan, John, *Irish Education, History and Structure* (Dublin: Institute of Public Administration, 1981).

Edwards, Amelia, *A Thousand Miles up the Nile* (London: Routledge and Sons, 1888).

Fitzpatrick, David, *Irish Emigration, 1801–1921* (Dundalk: Economic and Social History Society of Ireland, 1984).

Foster, David OSB, *Reading with God, Lectio Divina* (London & New York: Continuum International Publishing Group, 2005).

Hilpisch, Stephanus OSB, *History of Benedictine Nuns* (Minnesota: St John's Abbey Press, 1958).

Kyne, Sara, *Behind the Walls of Kylemore, A Visual Diary* (Privately published, 2010).

Lee, Dame Magdalen OSB, *By Strange Paths* (Kylemore: Kylemore Abbey Publications, 2002).

Logan, John (ed.), *Teachers' Union, the TUI and its forerunners, 1899–1994* (Dublin: A&A Farmar, 1999).

Lux-Sterritt, Laurence, *English Benedictine Nuns in Exile in the Seventeenth Century* (Manchester: Manchester University Press, 2017).

Moran, Gerard, *Sending Out Ireland's Poor: Assisted Emigration to North America in the Nineteenth Century* (Dublin: Four Courts Press, 2004).

Mulryan Moloney, Maeve, *Nineteenth-Century Elementary Education in the Archdiocese of Tuam* (Dublin and Portland OR: Irish Academic Press, 2001).

Raftery, Deirdre, Delaney, Catriona and Nowlan-Roebuck, Catherine, *Nano Nagle, the Life and the Legacy* (Kildare: Irish Academic Press, 2019).

Randles, Eileen, *Post-Primary Education in Ireland, 1957–70* (Dublin: Veritas, 1975).

Scannláin, Eibhlín Ní, *Land and the People: Land Uses and Population Change in North and West Connemara in the 19th Century* (Connemara: Connemara West plc and Dúchas, the Heritage Service, 1999).

Sheldon, J., *The German Army at Ypres 1914* (London: Pen & Sword Military, 2010).

Smith, Cyprian OSB, *The Path of Life* (York: Ampleforth Abbey Press,1995; reprinted 1996 & 2004).

Villiers-Tuthill, Kathleen, 'The Irish Benedictine Nuns: From Ypres to Kylemore' in Martin Browne OSB and Colmán Ó Clabaigh OSB, *The Irish Benedictines: A History* (Dublin: The Columba Press, 2005).

——————————, *History of Kylemore Castle & Abbey* (Kylemore: Kylemore Abbey Publications, 2002; 2013).

Waldron, Kieran, *Out of the Shadows, Emerging Secondary Schools in the Archdiocese of Tuam, 1940–69* (Tuam: Nordlaw Books, 2002).

Walsh, John, *The Politics of Expansion: The Transformation of Educational Policy in the Republic of Ireland, 1957–72* (Manchester: Manchester University Press, 2009).

VI. ARTICLES

Cavenagh, W.O., 'The Irish Benedictine nunnery at Ypres, Belgium', *The Journal of the Royal Society of Antiquaries of Ireland*, Fifth Series, 38:2 (30 June 1908).

Coonerty, Paula, 'The Presentation sisters and the education of "poor female children" in Limerick, 1837–1870', *The Old Limerick Journal* (Winter 1996).

Gill, Henry V., 'The Fate of the Irish Flag at Ypres', *Studies, An Irish Quarterly Review*, 8:29 (1919).

Kennedy, Kieran A. and Bruton, Richard, 'The Irish economy', *Economic and Financial Series*, 10 (1975).

Mansfield, Fr Brocard, 'A short-lived Royal Dublin foundation', *Dublin Historical Record*, 36:2 (March 1983).

Moran, Gerard, 'James Hack Tuke and his schemes for assisted emigration from the West of Ireland', *History Ireland*, May/June 2013.

Moylan, King, 'The district of Grangegorman: part III', *Dublin Historical Record*, 7:3 (June/August 1945).

Raftery, Deirdre, 'Rebels with a cause: obedience, resistance and convent life, 1800–1940', *History of Education*, 42:6 (2013).

VII. JOURNALS

Dublin Historical Record, 7:3 (June/August, 1945).

Dublin Historical Record, 36:2 (March, 1983).

Economic and Financial Series, 10 (1975).

History Ireland, May/June 2013.

History of Education, 42:6 (2013).

Studies, An Irish Quarterly Review, 8:29 (1919).

The Journal of the Royal Society of Antiquaries of Ireland, Fifth Series, 38:2 (30 June 1908).

The Old Limerick Journal (Winter 1996).

INDEX